PROGRAM DESIGN
WITH PSEUDOCODE

BROOKS/COLE SERIES IN COMPUTER SCIENCE

Program Design with Pseudocode
T.E. Bailey and Kris Lundgaard

BASIC: An Introduction to Computer Programming with the Apple
Robert J. Bent and George C. Sethares

BASIC: An Introduction to Computer Programming, Second Edition
Robert J. Bent and George C. Sethares

Business BASIC
Robert J. Bent and George C. Sethares

FORTRAN with Problem Solving: A Structured Approach
Robert J. Bent and George C. Sethares

Beginning BASIC
Keith Carver

Beginning Structured COBOL
Keith Carver

Structured COBOL for Microcomputers
Keith Carver

Learning BASIC Programming: A Systematic Approach
Howard Dachslager, Masato Hayashi, and Richard Zucker

Problem Solving and Structured Programming with ForTran 77
Martin O. Holoien and Ali Behforooz

Basic Business BASIC: Using Microcomputers
Peter Mears and Louis Raho

BROOKS/COLE SERIES IN COMPUTER EDUCATION

An Apple for the Teacher: Fundamentals of Instructional Computing
George Culp and Herbert Nickles

RUN: Computer Education
Dennis O. Harper and James H. Stewart

PROGRAM DESIGN WITH PSEUDOCODE

T. E. Bailey
University of Central Arkansas

Kris Lundgaard
Systematics, Inc.

Brooks/Cole Publishing Company
Monterey, California

Brooks/Cole Publishing Company
A Division of Wadsworth, Inc.

Printed in the United States of America
10 9 8 7 6 5 4 3 2 1

Library of Congress Cataloging in Publication Data

Bailey, T. E. (date)
  Program design with pseudocode.

  Includes index.
  1. Electronic digital computers—Programming.
I. Lundgaard, Kris (date)   . II. Title.
QA76.6.B327   1983   001.64'2   82-17802
ISBN 0-534-01361-9

Subject Editor: *Jim Leisy, Jr.*
Production Editor: *Marlene Thom*
Manuscript Editor: *Jonas Weisel*
Text and Cover Design: *Nancy Benedict*
Design Coordination: *Jamie Sue Brooks and Michele Judge*
Illustrations: *Brenda Booth*
Typesetting: *Omegatype Typography, Inc., Champaign, Illinois*

PREFACE

When faced with a problem to be solved with a computer, many beginning students seem to have difficulty knowing where and how to start. This book presents a method of problem solving that helps programmers determine the operations necessary for transforming the given information into the required information. The method utilizes Input/Process/Output (IPO) diagrams, which are displayed extensively throughout the book.

A second objective of this book is to present effective methods of program design and modular construction with IPO diagrams and pseudocode, using sequence, selection, and repetition units. This will aid students in learning from the outset good program design and structure.

A third objective is to present fundamental algorithms and concepts used in computer solutions.

We have used flowcharts in some early chapters as a pedagogical tool to help the reader visualize solutions. However, we have not used flowcharts as a tool for problem solving and program design. IPO diagrams and pseudocode are simpler to use and are more likely to result in well-designed programs.

Although the problem-solving and program-design techniques presented in this book are certainly not the only ones available, they are particularly effective for beginning programmers.

We intend this book to be used as a complementary textbook for any beginning programming course, regardless of the computer language used. A language manual or textbook must be used for presenting a specific language in which pseudocode programs will be implemented.

We wish to thank Mike Folk and Barbara Pass for advice during the development of this material and for testing it in the classroom.

We would also like to thank the following reviewers for their insightful comments and contribution to the manuscript: Charles P. Downey, University of Nebraska at Omaha; Alan C. Jost, United States Air Force Academy; and Doug Smith, Naval Postgraduate School. In addition, we thank Jonas Weisel for correcting the infelicities of our writing and Marlene Thom for providing invaluable assistance during the production process.

T. E. Bailey
Kris Lundgaard

CONTENTS

PROGRAM DESIGN
WITH PSEUDOCODE

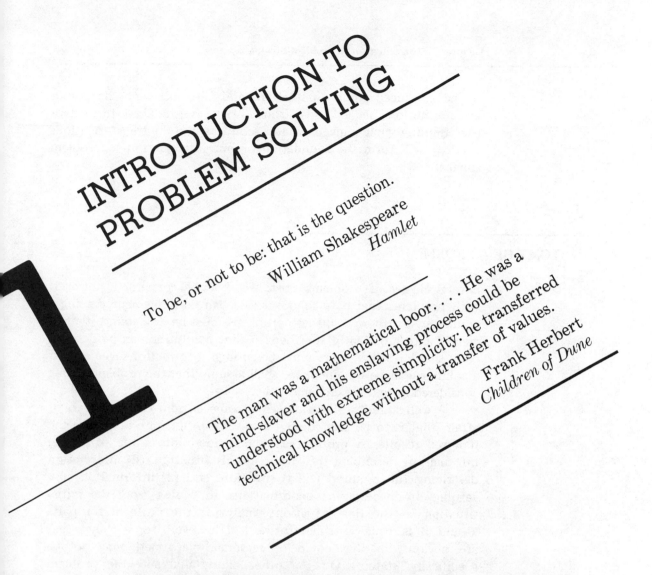

INTRODUCTION TO PROBLEM SOLVING

To be, or not to be: that is the question.

William Shakespeare
Hamlet

The man was a mathematical boor. . . . He was a mind-slaver and his enslaving process could be understood with extreme simplicity: he transferred technical knowledge without a transfer of values.

Frank Herbert
Children of Dune

Problem solving is perhaps the greatest difficulty that most students face in computer programming. For our purposes, we shall define problem solving as a procedure, specifically the procedure of determining the solution to a problem and stating that solution in a specific programming language.

There are numerous approaches to the correct solution to a problem. However, the number of clear, efficient, and easily defined approaches may be limited, and we shall limit our discussion of problem solving to a single approach. Our approach is a general method that is especially useful for computer applications.

Our approach requires a careful analysis of the problem in order to determine what information is initially given, what is to be produced upon completion, and the necessary changes or transformations needed to go from start to finish. These three steps (determining what is given, what is required, and the transformations needed) will form the foundation of our introduction to problem solving.

ANATOMY OF A PROBLEM

Several classes of problems exist. We shall be concerned, however, with problems that have solutions that can be implemented using a computer. Furthermore, these problems must be well stated—that is, clearly and sufficiently specified so that a solution can be derived; or in simpler terms, there must be enough information given so that a solution can be obtained. We shall assume that the problems being considered have these characteristics.

A well-stated problem describes some current or initial state of affairs that is to be transformed into some other state of affairs—the required results. A problem can be divided into three parts: (1) information describing the given (initial) situation, (2) information describing the required (final) situation, and (3) information concerning the necessary transformations for going from the initial situation to the final situation. Analyzing the problem for parts 1 and 2 is usually straightforward. (However, some things that are obvious, or that could be reasonably assumed, may not be specifically stated.) On the other hand, analyzing the problem for part 3 may not be straightforward. Usually not all of the transformations will be specified; perhaps none will be. Transformations are often only implied within the context of the problem, or they may be left entirely to the inventiveness and ingenuity of the problem solver.

A quick rule of thumb may help to identify the three parts of a problem. The given and required information, which is normally descriptive, is often stated in nouns and adjectives; transformations, which are typically actions, are stated in verbs and adverbs. This concept is summarized in the following question: What must be done to change (action, verb) what is given (descriptive, noun) into what is required (descriptive, noun)?

Example 1   Statement of problem: I am at the corner of Tenth Street and C Avenue, and I must go to the store at Fifteenth Street and L Avenue.

Part 1   Initial situation: "Tenth and C" implies a place or location (noun). This location is described very specifically: Tenth Street and C Avenue.

Part 2   Final situation: "Fifteenth and L" also implies a location, which is described as Fifteenth Street and L Avenue.

Part 3   Transformations: The action stated in the problem is *go*. The idea is to change location, and this is accomplished by going, moving, or transporting my body. (Notice that how this action is accomplished is not specified. The how involves tools and operations, which will be discussed in the next section.)

The analysis of the problem has produced the following result, which can be summarized in a simple diagram.

Given	Transformations	Required
Location at Tenth and C.	Change locations (go).	Location at Fifteenth and L.

This simple example clearly illustrates the initial steps of problem solving: breaking down the problem into its three fundamental parts. This process must be done accurately and completely, using only what is specified in the statement of the problem, before attempting any further analysis. An important feature of the analysis performed so far is that it represents a generalized overview of the problem and lacks details. This is exactly what is required from the preliminary analysis. By analogy to human anatomy, the preliminary analysis takes notice only of the head, trunk, arms, and legs.

TOOLS AND OPERATIONS

After a problem has been dissected into its three parts, its general anatomy becomes apparent. Next, we must perform a further dissection of the general parts in order to reveal the detailed anatomy—

hands, feet, fingers, toes, knees, elbows, and so on—and the order in which they are connected. The major concern in this step is the dissection of the transformations into detailed, precise steps. Although we ignored the *how* of transformations in the last section, we shall now scrutinize part 3 of the analysis and examine tools and their uses (operations).

For example 1, the following diagram summarized the solution:

Given	Transformations	Required
Location at Tenth and C.	Change locations (go).	Location at Fifteenth and L.

As explained in the previous section, the required action is to change location; nothing, however, is stated regarding how this is to be done. Nonetheless, we might reasonably assume that someone intelligent enough to read the problem can certainly determine a way of going from Tenth and C to Fifteenth and L. Therefore, the process of going is left as an open choice. One's reasoning might proceed as follows: In order to go, I must have some means of movement. A basic operation in the human experience is go, and I know how to do this by selection of appropriate tools. Suppose that I have the following tools available: feet, bicycle, and car. I know how to operate each. Which tool shall I choose? That will depend on several considerations, such as: Is it raining? Do I have limited time? Will I be carrying a large load? In any event, it is left to my own ingenuity to choose the appropriate tool (feet, bicycle, or car) and use it (walk, ride, or drive) correctly to transport my body from the given location to the required location.

Since an intelligent choice of a tool and its operation is obvious in this case, there is no need to expand the middle column of the diagram. "Change location" and "go" describe implicitly and as simply as possible the required transformation.

Still, the process of going from Tenth and C to Fifteenth and L is not completely described by the selection of a tool. Even though one may choose to walk, he or she could still raise questions about how to go to the right place—for example, when and which ways to turn and how far to go. The development of step 3 (analyzing the necessary transformations for going from the initial situation to the final situation) is still incomplete.

ORDERED STEPS FOR PERFORMING
TRANSFORMATIONS

Certain additional details and ordered steps must be followed in order to ensure a correct arrival at Fifteenth and L. Even though we have allowed the *go* to include implicitly a tool and its operation, we have neglected another very important aspect of going, since *go* also implies direction. In which direction must the feet, bicycle, or car be pointed? Thus, there is a systematic and ordered sequence of activities involved in the going. This sequence, which is called the *process*, consists of a set of detailed directions or instructions. Determining the process is the final stage in step 3 of problem analysis, and it is probably the most difficult aspect of problem solving. The process must be synthesized by answering the question "Precisely how can I make use of the tool(s), which, of course, I know how to operate, to transform the initial situation into the final situation?" For example, one might have wood (given); a saw, hammer, screwdriver, screws, nails, and glue (tools); and the knowledge to use them (operations). Nevertheless, he or she cannot produce a wooden table (required) without a set of directions for building a table (ordered steps, process). This same idea can be expressed in terms of the problem stated in example 1. One is at Tenth and C (given) and has a car (tool) and the skill to drive it (operation), but he or she cannot go to Fifteenth and L (required) without a set of instructions detailing which direction and how far to go, where to turn, and so on (process).

How can these details be inferred from the statement of the problem? Since they are not stated explicitly, they must be inferred based on common sense, certain well-known tools and operations, and perhaps some assumptions. In this case, the streets identified by numbers give a clue that numbered streets go east-west or north-south. It really doesn't matter in solving this problem which points of the compass are used, so let us assume east-west. In the same manner, the streets identified by letters allow us to assume that they too are ordered and that, if numbered streets are east-west, lettered streets are north-south. In other words, the streets of the city are laid out on a rectangular grid, and they are ordered by number and alphabet. Once this is recognized, the process of going becomes straightforward. One can, for example, go on C to Fifteenth, turn onto Fifteenth, and go to L, as shown for path A in Figure 1-1. But is this the only way to go? Of course not! One could just as well go on Tenth to L and go to Fifteenth (path B). There are, in fact, many alternative paths, some of which are shown in Figure 1-1. All are equally correct, but two of them (paths A and B) are simpler than the rest. Arbitrarily choosing path B, let us expand the diagram that describes the solution into the one shown in Figure 1-2.

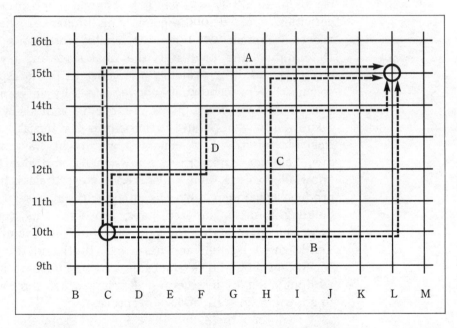

Figure 1-1.   Some pathways from Tenth and C to Fifteenth and L.

Given	Transformations	Required
Location at Tenth and C.	1. Go on Tenth to L. 2. Turn onto L. 3. Go to Fifteenth.	Location at Fifteenth and L.

Figure 1-2.   Going from Tenth and C to Fifteenth and L by path B (Figure 1-1).

When inferring the information summarized in Figure 1-1, we made some important assumptions that have not yet been mentioned. All streets are through streets. Each pathway is equally pleasant. We have not considered such things as the number of stop signs and traffic lights, traffic density, smoothness of the streets, or width of the roadways. Furthermore, it was assumed that the direction to go toward Fifteenth or L was known. (Can you think of other assumptions? What if there are one-way streets?)

A process for going from Tenth and C to Fifteenth and L has now been developed, but it still needs additional refinement. What happens if one goes the wrong direction at a turn? What happens if one does not know which direction to go to Fifteenth or L? A better statement of the process takes these eventualities into account. For example, step 1 of the process, go on Tenth to L, could be expanded as follows to include the possibility of going the wrong direction: Go on Tenth to the next street. If the next street is B, turn around; then go on Tenth to L. (Can we assume that "turn around" is a basic operation that everyone knows how to do?) The process should also include a statement of when to stop the process—that is, when the transformations are completed. These changes are shown in Figure 1-3.

Given	Transformations	Required
Location at Tenth and C.	1. Go on Tenth to next street.	Location at Fifteenth and L.
	2. If next street is B, then turn around.	
	3. Go on Tenth to L.	
	4. Turn left onto L.	
	5. Go to next street.	
	6. If next street is Ninth, then turn around.	
	7. Go on L to Fifteenth.	
	8. Stop.	

Figure 1-3.   Going from Tenth and C to Fifteenth and L, general solution.

Since there are many processes that will work in the solution to this problem, the one shown is an arbitrary choice. Figure 1-4 shows an equally correct variation.

Given	Transformations	Required
Location at Tenth and C.	1. Go on Tenth to next street.	Location at Fifteenth and L.
	2. If next street is D, then go on Tenth to L; otherwise, turn around and go on Tenth to L.	
	3. Turn right onto L.	
	4. Go to next street.	
	5. If next street is Eleventh, then go on L to Fifteenth; otherwise turn around and go on L to Fifteenth.	
	6. Stop.	

Figure 1-4. Going from Tenth and C to Fifteenth and L, alternate general solution.

Based on our assumptions, the process is now complete. In fact, the solution has been clearly and unambiguously stated so that anyone can perform the transition from Tenth and C to Fifteenth and L. It can be tested for correctness by working it by hand, using Figure 1-1.

The analysis of any problem is an iterative, or repetitive, procedure. In the development of step 3, for example, three "passes" were required. At the completion of a pass, each step of the process must be analyzed further in order to determine whether it adequately considers all reasonably possible events that might occur as the process is performed. (In our example, this included the possibility of turning the wrong way at an intersection and starting in the wrong direction.) Iteration may also be required in the development of steps 1 and 2, since more detail may be necessary in them as step 3 is developed.

FLOWCHARTS

A *flowchart* is a useful tool for visualizing a set of transformations. Flowcharts consist of certain symbols connected by arrows. Figure 1-5 shows three commonly used symbols and their meanings.

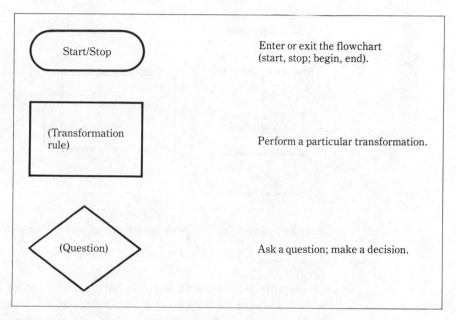

Figure 1-5.   Some common flowchart symbols.

The arrows connecting flowchart symbols have two meanings:

1. They show the order in which the transformations are to be performed.
2. They show the pathway, or "flow," of given information going into a symbol and required information coming out.

Figure 1-6 shows arrows attached to the symbols to indicate the flow of information.

The *start* symbol can have only one arrow coming out since it is the beginning of the flowchart. Similarly, the *stop* symbol can have only one arrow going in since it is the end of the flowchart. The *transformation* symbol has one arrow going in and one arrow coming out. The *question* symbol has only one arrow going in, but it must have two (or more, in some cases) coming out—one for each possible answer to the question (usually yes or no).

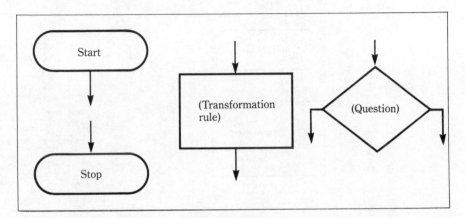

Figure 1-6.   The "flow" or pathways into and out of flowchart symbols.

Figure 1-7 contains a flowchart for the set of transformations in the diagram in Figure 1-3. Each transformation symbol has a transformation rule written within the symbol. Each question symbol has a question written inside it; the possible answers to the question (yes or no) are written on the corresponding outgoing arrows.

The advantage of the flowchart is that it provides a visual aid that emphasizes the ordered flow of information through a set of transformations. Disadvantages are that the flowchart is a bit cumbersome and takes up considerably more space than a statement of the transformations in ordinary English. These disadvantages of flowcharting will eventually make flowcharting of large problems impractical. However, because it helps to visualize solutions and it concretely demonstrates simple computer logic, we will often ask you to construct flowcharts for solutions.

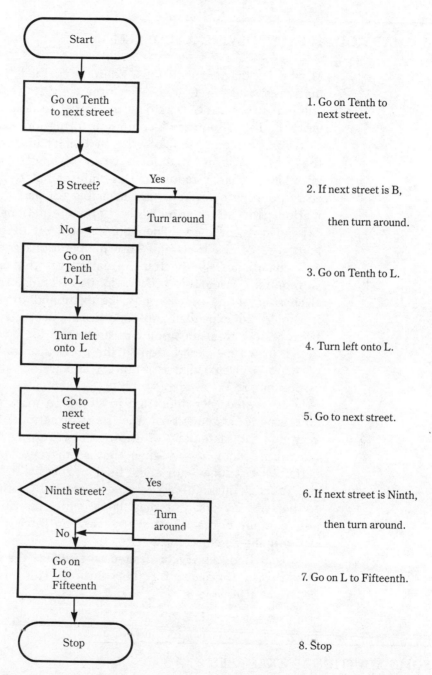

1. Go on Tenth to next street.

2. If next street is B,

   then turn around.

3. Go on Tenth to L.

4. Turn left onto L.

5. Go to next street.

6. If next street is Ninth,

   then turn around.

7. Go on L to Fifteenth.

8. Stop

Figure 1-7. Flowchart for the transformations in Figure 1-3. The transformations from Figure 1-3 are stated to the right of their respective flowchart symbols.

SUMMARY OF STEPS IN SOLVING A PROBLEM

Mark off a diagram with three columns entitled "Given," "Transformations," and "Required." Perform step 1: write in the "Given" column information describing the initial situation. Perform step 2: write in the "Required" column information describing the final situation. Perform step 3: write in the "Transformations" column the general actions that must be performed to transform what is given into what is required. Determine what tools, including their corresponding operations, are available for performing the transformations; the information in the "Transformations" column may be expanded accordingly. Then construct a set of ordered steps that make use of the tools and known operations and describe exactly and unambiguously the transformation of what is given into what is required. Place this process in the "Transformations" column. Each step of the process must be examined to determine whether it should be expanded into additional steps. This procedure may be repeated from any point as necessary for developing sufficient detail. The final description of the process must be stated in terms of what is given, what is required, and well-known operations corresponding to the available tools.

It is especially important in step 3 to work from a very broad and general statement of the transformations to a detailed and very specific statement of the process. Testing for correctness by hand can occur at any time that seems appropriate, but it must certainly be done with the "final" process. If an error is found, the process must, of course, be corrected. If the process appears to be without error, it may be accepted as final—though it may still contain errors. (Testing by two or three people will help in determining its correctness.)

If it is necessary or desired to visualize the solution, you may construct a flowchart for the solution. This may be done either before or after step 3.

SOME ADDITIONAL EXAMPLES

The problems selected for illustration are simple, and their solutions are straightforward and intuitive. This has been done so that the problem itself does not become a barrier to your understanding of the steps in its analysis and solution.

Example 2   (This problem illustrates a simple case in which step 3 of the analysis does not require additional refinement.)

Statement of problem: What is the length in centimeters of the following line?

Part 1   Initial situation: We are given a specific line (noun).

Part 2   Final situation: We want to know the length (noun) of the line. A special constraint has been placed on the result in that the length must be expressed in centimeters.

Part 3   Transformations: There is no action as such specified in the problem, but "What is the length?" implies an action—that is, measure (verb). Once again, the how of measuring is not expressed.

What we have done so far can be summarized in the following diagram:

Given	*Transformations*	*Required*
A line.	Measure in centimeters.	Length in centimeters.

Step 3, however, may not be complete. How is the measuring to take place? No tool is specified, but the constraint "in centimeters" certainly suggests some kind of ruler marked in centimeters—a meter stick, for example, or a short centimeter ruler. The operation of the measuring device is also unspecified but assumed; using a meter stick for measuring is a well-known operation—at least, it should be. Is it necessary to make additional steps to describe the measuring process? Probably not, since the entire process should be well known.

What if it is not well known? What if one is trying to give instructions to a very young child? Then the process cannot be assumed to be well known and must be stated step by step in terms of tools and operations that are known to a young child. Although this is an important point to be considered, there is no need for us to go into it further. "Measure in centimeters" is assumed to be a well-known process for an adult.

The diagram will, therefore, be used in its present form without further expansion, though placing "stop" after "measure in centimeters" is appropriate.

Example 3 Statement of problem: Express the temperature 85 degrees Fahrenheit (F) in degrees centigrade (C).

Part 1 Initial situation: We have a temperature of 85 degrees Fahrenheit.

Part 2 Final situation: We want the temperature in degrees centigrade.

Part 3 Transformations: The only verb in the statement of the problem is *express*, which does not seem to give any clues regarding the necessary transformations. It takes little effort, however, to realize that the transformation involves a conversion from one set of units to another. Therefore, the action is "convert," but the how is unspecified and thus to be worked out. In other words, some tool must be found to accomplish the conversion; the tool is left to the choice of the problem solver. Actually there are at least two ways to convert from degrees Fahrenheit to degrees centigrade: by use of a conversion table and by use of an algebraic formula. Therefore, we must find one of these tools before proceeding. Suppose that we find the formula

$$^\circ C = \frac{5(^\circ F - 32)}{9}$$

If we assume that the operation of this tool—that is, the necessary skills for evaluation of the algebraic expression—is well known, the diagram will be as shown in Figure 1-8.

Given	*Transformations*	*Required*
85° F.	Compute degrees centigrade by evaluating the expression $\frac{5(^\circ F - 32)}{9}$	Degrees centigrade.

Figure 1-8.   Converting degrees Fahrenheit to degrees centigrade, using algebraic notation.

On the other hand, if algebraic operations are not assumed to be well known, the process can be described in detail using only the well-known operations of arithmetic (see Figure 1-9).

Given	Transformations	Required
85° F.	1. Subtract 32 from degrees Fahrenheit.	Degrees centigrade.
	2. Multiply result from step 1 by 5.	
	3. Divide result from step 2 by 9.	
	4. Stop.	

Figure 1-9. Converting degrees Fahrenheit to degrees centigrade using well-known arithmetic operations.

The term *well-known operations* has been used throughout these examples without discussing its meaning, but more will be said about it in the next chapter.

EXERCISES

1. Construct diagrams that describe the solutions to the following problems:
   a. Cut a round pizza into eight equal pieces.
   b. Put on shoes and socks.
   c. Write a letter to a friend.
   d. Set an alarm clock for seven o'clock.
   e. Construct flowcharts for a–d.

2. Identify the tools and operations in the preceding problems.

3. Consider the specific order of operation in the exercise 1 problems.

4. In example 2 we assumed that measuring is a well-known operation. Suppose that measuring is not well known to a child and that you must describe the process in terms of operations that are well known to him or her—such as counting marks, aligning the ruler and

its marks with the line, and recognizing the centimeter marks. Construct a diagram containing a process for measuring the line, using basic operations appropriate for a child. You may or may not wish to use the basic operations listed; you may wish to use additional ones, but they must be clearly defined and well known. If possible, test your process on a child. At least test it on someone else who can pretend to be ignorant of how to measure. If you can test it on a child, be prepared for some surprises!

5. Tying a shoelace is a well-known operation for an adult. But suppose that you must describe the process to someone (a child perhaps) who does not know a shoelace from a pretzel. Construct a diagram showing a solution to the problem: "tie a shoelace." You will have to select and clearly define a set of basic operations around which the process can be developed. (Here are a few hints: How is a loop formed? How are the ends pulled so that they are tightened? How is one end passed under the other? How are the hands and fingers, which are tools, used?) When you have completed the diagram and tested it yourself, test it on someone else, making sure that he or she follows the procedure literally and uses only those basic operations that you have defined.

6. Construct a diagram that describes the school enrollment process.

7. Construct a diagram that describes the solution to the problem: "find a book in the library."

8. Construct a diagram that describes the process of getting gasoline at a self-service station.

9. Construct a diagram that describes the solution to the problem: "mail a letter."

10. Construct a diagram that describes the solution to the following problem. Mr. Math E. Mattox has just purchased a lot in the city. The lot is square, each side measures 300 feet, and the entire lot is bordered by streets. His problem is to divide the lot into rectangular sections, each with 100 feet of frontage.

11. Construct a flowchart for the set of transformations in Figure 1-4.

12. When counting change, one starts with the largest coin, counting out one less than the number that gives an amount greater than the change, and proceeds in the same manner to the smallest coin. Construct a diagram that describes the counting of change, assuming

that a sufficient number of quarters, dimes, nickels, and pennies is available.

13. Identify the tools and well-known operations in exercises 6–12. (Assume that we are dealing with adults of reasonable intelligence and a high school education.)

14. Construct a flowchart for exercise 12.

15. A particular TV set has two channel-selector dials. The upper dial is for channels 2–13 and also has a *U* setting, which activates the lower (UHF) dial for channels 14–83. Construct a diagram that describes the selection of any channel.

16. Construct a flowchart for exercise 15.

17. A particular TV set has a 10-key (digits 0–9) channel selector. The first key pressed is for the tens digit and the second for the units digit. Construct a diagram for the selection of any channel. What happens if one enters an invalid channel—that is, one not included in the range 2–83?

18. Construct a flowchart for exercise 17.

19. Construct a diagram describing the use of a touch-tone telephone for reaching any party. The rules are as follows.

> If the call is local, key in the number.
>
> If the call is not local but to a party whose area code is the same as yours, key in 1 followed by the number.
>
> If the call is to a party having a different area code from yours, key in 1 followed by the area code followed by the number.

20. Construct a flowchart for exercise 19.

2 PROBLEM SOLVING WITH A COMPUTER

When you think you know something, that is a most perfect barrier against learning.

Frank Herbert
God Emperor of Dune

It is no use doing what you like; you have got to like what you do.

Winston S. Churchill
Painting as a Pastime

A generalized concept of problem solving was presented in the last chapter, which discussed tools and operations. When the solution to a problem is to be implemented on a computer, the computer itself becomes (in the broadest sense) the tool; thus, the solution must be stated in terms of the set of operations that the computer can perform. This puts certain constraints on the problem solver, who must define the tool and the set of operations explicitly. We shall begin stating solutions in computer-related terms in this chapter.

ALGORITHMS

Many people have defined and discussed the word *algorithm*. For simplicity's sake, we shall use an elementary and intuitive definition.

Process was used in the last chapter for the set of detailed, unambiguous, and ordered instructions developed to describe the transformations necessary to go from the initial (given) situation to the final (required) situation. The processes developed were actually algorithms. Certain properties of an algorithm became evident:

1. It must be sufficiently detailed to describe the transformations necessary to solve the problem.

2. It must be unambiguous, so that anyone can perform the transformations correctly every time.

3. It must always give the same results for the same initial situation.

4. It must give correct results in all cases.

A process must meet these criteria to be considered an algorithm; in computer programming the process used to solve a problem must be an algorithm.

MORE ON OPERATIONS

We said much in the last chapter about operations and indicated that they must be "well known." An algorithm may be thought of as simply a series of one or more well-known operations. Each well-known operation must, therefore, meet the requirements of an algorithm. Now that we know the properties of an algorithm, we can examine specific operations to determine whether they are well known by judging them according to the properties of algorithms.

Consider the arithmetic operation *add* as an example. Is *add* well known? Suppose that the problem is to add two numbers. A diagram summarizing the solution can be constructed as follows:

Given	Transformations	Required
Two numbers.	Add first number to second.	Sum.

By applying the criteria for an algorithm, we can determine the appropriateness of the single operation *add*.

1. Is *add* sufficiently detailed to describe the necessary transformations? Yes. We know how to add two numbers.

2. Is it unambiguous? Yes.

3. Does it always give the same result? Yes.

4. Does it give the correct result? Yes. (We assume that the addition is done correctly.)

Add meets the criteria and qualifies as a well-known operation. If any question had been answered no, we would have had to break down *add* into simpler steps, each being a well-known operation.

By meeting these criteria, *add* is also a single-step algorithm. Common algorithms often become basic operations that are well known once they have been established and verified. Algorithms such as extracting the square root, computing simple interest, and plotting a graph are algorithms that may be considered well-known operations once they become familiar to the user. The distinction between algorithms and well-known operations depends much on the user's knowledge.

To a child first learning, addition must be described in simpler operations, such as counting. Once addition is mastered, it becomes a basic operation. Most of us have forgotten how we learned to add or even how we add; we just do it! What was once an algorithm for addition has become a well-known operation.

AN ALGORITHM FOR FINDING THE LARGEST NUMBER

Imagine a stack of cards with a number written on each. The problem is to find the largest of these numbers.

The solution to this problem is trivial if the number of cards is small. If there are five cards, one could find the largest number by a quick glance at the cards. Different people would perform this task differently, without having to think about what they are doing. (Would these intuitive processes be algorithms?)

If there are 1000 cards, however, a quick solution would not be possible. Instead, there must be some systematic process (algorithm) for solving the problem in an orderly fashion and ensuring a correct result. The algorithm for solving this problem must work for any number of cards.

The algorithm can be developed, assuming the following set of well-known operations:

Remove top card from stack.

Determine whether stack is empty.

Copy number from top card to piece of paper.

Determine larger of two numbers.

Given: A stack of cards with a number on each. (Paper and pencil are assumed from the third well-known operation.)

Required: Largest number, written on paper.

Transformations: A list of things that must be done can be compiled with no regard for logical order.

Copy the number from the top card onto the paper.

When the number on the top card is larger than the last number on the paper, copy the larger number onto the paper.

Stop when stack is empty.

Remove the top card from the stack.

Repeat appropriate steps until all cards are used.

Although this list is not necessarily complete, these items, which result from a preliminary analysis, give us something to work with. They must be refined and placed into logical order. An observation that can help to establish the proper order is that we are recording, or saving, the largest number found thus far; each time a larger number is encountered, it must be saved on paper.

The process resulting from this analysis is shown in Figure 2-1, and the flowchart is shown in Figure 2-2.

Is the process an algorithm? Yes.

1. It is sufficiently detailed to describe the necessary transformations.

2. It is unambiguous.

3. It gives the same result for the same set of cards.

4. It gives the correct result every time for any set of cards or numbers.

Given	Transformations	Required
Stack of cards with number on each card.	1. Copy number from top card onto paper. 2. Remove top card from stack. 3. If stack is empty, then stop. 4. Otherwise, compare number on top card with number on paper. 5. If number on top card is larger, then copy number from card onto paper. 6. Go to step 2.	Largest number on paper.

Figure 2-1. *Finding the largest number in a stack of cards.*

(It should be pointed out that we have not proved that the last statement is true. We can see, however, that it should work for any set of numbers if it works for several test cases.)

Are there other ways to construct the algorithm for this problem? Yes, several. One different way will be presented in Chapter 4.

An important question to raise at this point is, "Will the algorithm work for a null stack of cards?" (A *null stack* is one that contains no cards initially.) If you test it, you will find that it will not work. The next question is, "Should it?" The answer to that question depends on the needs of the user. We will assume that "a stack of cards" implies that the stack is not null; therefore, the answer is no.

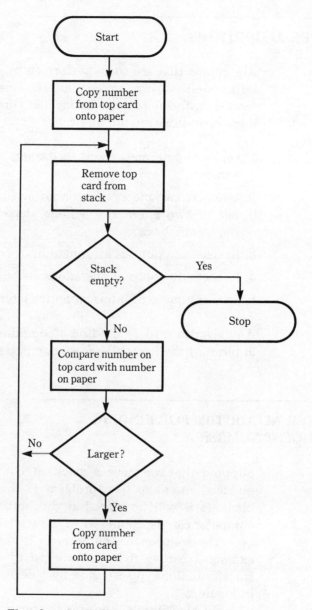

Figure 2-2.   Flowchart for finding the largest number in a stack of cards.

COMPUTER ALGORITHMS

Algorithms that are to be performed by computers must be stated in terms well known to computers. One must, therefore, become familiar with the few operations that computers can perform. Five of these operations are the following:

1. Perform arithmetic—add, subtract, multiply, and divide two numbers.

2. Compare two pieces of information (including numbers) and select one of two alternative actions, depending upon the outcome of the comparison.

3. Receive and put out information.

4. Repeat any group of operations.

5. Save any piece of information for later use.

Any algorithm to be used on a computer, therefore, must be stated in terms of the five well-known computer operations.

COMPUTER ALGORITHM FOR FINDING THE LARGEST NUMBER

Suppose that we have a stack of computer cards with a number punched on each. The problem is to find the largest number. A blank card will be placed at the bottom of the stack so that the computer can determine when the stack is empty.

The solution to the problem is essentially the same as the one examined earlier that was worked by hand. We can use the same transformations, placed side by side for comparison. This is shown in Figure 2-3.

An algorithm for solving the problem with a computer is shown in Figure 2-4.

This construction of the algorithm is not the only possible one, but it serves our purpose well. Is it an algorithm? If you apply the four properties of algorithms to it, you will see that it is.

Transformations (by hand)	Transformations (by computer)
1. Copy number from top card onto paper.	1. Get number from first card. 2. Save that number.
2. Remove top card from stack.	3. Repeat the following operations: a. Get new number from next card.

3. If stack is empty,
 	
   then stop.
	b. If card is blank, then
	     (1) write saved number.
	     (2) Stop.

4. Otherwise, compare number on top card with number on paper.	Otherwise (1) compare new number with number saved.
5. If number on top card is larger, then copy number from card onto paper.	(2) If new number is larger, then save new number.
6. Go to step 2.	

Figure 2-3. *Comparison of the processes for finding the largest number by hand and by computer. (Step 6 on the left side corresponds to "Repeat the following operations" in step 3 on the right side.)*

Given	Transformations	Required

Stack of cards with number on each card.	1. Get number from first card.
	
	 2. Save that number.
	
	 3. Repeat the following operations:
	   a. Get new number from next card.
	   b. If card is blank, then
	     (1) write saved number.
	     (2) Stop.
	   Otherwise
	   (1) compare new number with number saved.
	   (2) If new number is larger, then save new number.
		Largest number.

Figure 2-4. *Computer algorithm for finding the largest number.*

The format of the transformations may look a bit strange. This is a hint of things to come. The format closely resembles the format of computer programs. This format emphasizes two of the well-known computer operations—compare two numbers and repeat a group of operations.

It should be obvious from the computer algorithm that steps a and b are to be repeated, in that order. These steps, therefore, are indented under step 3 to show clearly what is to be repeated. Step 3b corresponds to the operation of comparing two numbers. A comparison is implied by "if card is blank," which must be followed by two alternative actions, "then" and "otherwise." The two alternative actions are shown clearly by indentation.

The "blank card" referred to in step 3b is known as a *trailer card*, which is used to determine when a process such as repetition is to stop. The concept and technique will be more fully developed in the chapter on repetition, Chapter 4.

EUCLID'S ALGORITHM

Euclid's algorithm for finding the greatest common divisor of two numbers is stated as follows:

Divide the smaller number into the larger. If the remainder is not zero, replace the original two numbers by the remainder and the smaller of the two numbers, and repeat the division. Eventually the remainder will be zero, in which case the smaller number is the greatest common divisor.

This may seem rather mathematical, but really the concept and algorithm are simple. No advanced understanding of mathematics is necessary; it is a simple exercise in elementary arithmetic.

For example, the greatest common divisor of 8 and 12 is 4; 4 is the largest number that can be divided into both 8 and 12 with a remainder of 0. Euclid's algorithm can be applied to 8 and 12 as follows:

1. Divide the smaller number (divisor) into the larger (dividend).

$$
\begin{array}{r}
1 \\
8 \overline{\smash{\big)}\ 12} \\
8 \\
\hline
4
\end{array}
$$

Divisor   8   12   Dividend

1   Quotient

8

4   Remainder

2. If the remainder is not 0 (it is 4), replace the two original numbers with the remainder and the smaller of the two numbers.

    The new numbers are 4 (the remainder) and 8 (the smaller of the two original numbers).

3. Repeat the division. (Divide the smaller number into the larger.)

$$
\begin{array}{r}
2 \\
4 \overline{\smash{\big)}\ 8} \\
8 \\
\hline
0
\end{array}
$$

0   Remainder

4. Eventually the remainder will be 0 (it is). The smaller number is then the greatest common divisor.

    4 is the greatest common divisor.

Euclid's algorithm produced the expected result, 4, when the numbers are 8 and 12.

Now we shall construct a computer algorithm that uses Euclid's algorithm to find the greatest common divisor. We shall begin with an important simplifying assumption: the two numbers will always be given in ascending order (smaller followed by the larger), so that we may be able to divide the first into the second, eliminating the need for an extra step to compare the two numbers.

Given: Two numbers in ascending order.

Required: Greatest common divisor.

Transformations: The numbers must be entered into the computer in ascending order. The larger number is then divided by the smaller, and the remainder is compared to zero. When it is zero, the process is complete, and the computer must put out the smaller number as the answer. If the remainder is not zero, the smaller of the original numbers (the divisor) must be replaced by the remainder, and the larger (the dividend) must be replaced by the smaller (the divisor). The larger is divided by the smaller again. These transformations must be stated in terms of the five computer operations.

Figure 2-5 is the diagram showing the solution.

Given	Transformations	Required

Two numbers, the smaller followed by the larger.	1. Read the smaller number and the larger number.
	
	2. Repeat the following operations:
	  a. Find the remainder of the larger divided by the smaller.
	  b. If remainder is zero, then
	    (1) put out smaller number (divisor).
	    (2) Stop.
	  Otherwise
	    (1) save remainder.
	    (2) Save smaller number (divisor).
		Greatest common divisor.

Figure 2-5. Finding the greatest common divisor by computer (Euclid's algorithm).

This awkward statement of the process is too wordy and imprecise for computer solution. Since computer languages allow us to give numbers *names*, we have a simpler way to identify the smaller and larger numbers. (Such names are also called labels, identifiers, and variables.) Recall computer operation 5: save any piece of information for later use. When information is saved, we need to give it a name so that we can easily refer to it when it is used. (How the computer uses names to refer to information is discussed in Chapter 3, but it is not necessary to turn to that discussion at this point.) The process can be refined by using names. Figure 2-6 illustrates this.

Given	Transformations	Required

Two numbers, the smaller followed by the larger.	1. Read two numbers, J (smaller) and K (larger).
	
	2. Repeat the following operations:
	  a. Find the remainder R of K divided by J.
	  b. If R is zero, then
	    (1) put out J.
	    (2) Stop.
	  Otherwise
	    (1) save J in K.
	    (2) save R in J.
		Greatest common divisor.

Figure 2-6.   *Simplified process for Euclid's algorithm, using the* repeat *operation.*

FLOWCHART SYMBOLS FOR COMPUTER OPERATIONS

Five computer operations have been presented in this chapter:

1. Perform arithmetic—add, subtract, multiply, and divide two numbers.

2. Compare two pieces of information (including numbers) and select one of two alternative actions, depending upon the outcome of the comparison.

3. Receive and put out information.

4. Repeat any group of operations.

5. Save any piece of information for later use.

We use the transformation symbol (rectangle) for operations 1 and 5. We use the question symbol (diamond) for operation 2. For operation 3, we will use the input/output symbol, which is a parallelogram. These symbols are shown in Figure 2-7.

Operation 4 requires a combination of the symbols in Figure 2-7. A flowchart for Euclid's algorithm (Figure 2-6), which includes a *repeat* operation, is shown in Figure 2-8. The *repeat* operation is indicated by an arrow going from the box containing "Save R in J" to the box containing "Find remainder."

PERFORMING A TRACE OF AN ALGORITHM

When the solution diagram is constructed, the algorithm must be tested for correctness. This is accomplished by a *hand simulation*.

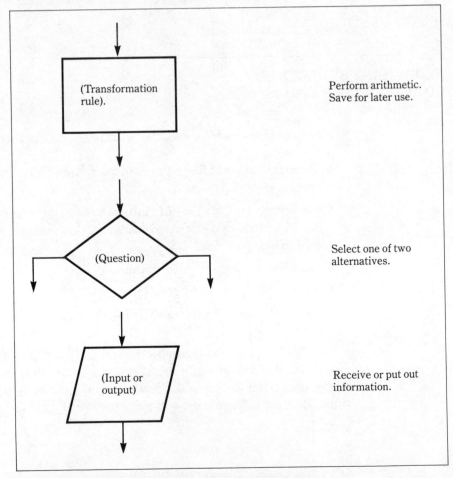

Figure 2-7.   *Flowchart symbols for computer operations.*

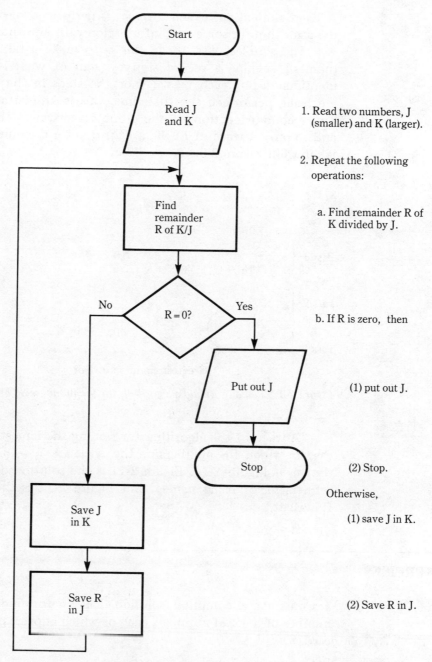

Figure 2-8.   Flowchart for Euclid's algorithm.

1. Read two numbers, J (smaller) and K (larger).

2. Repeat the following operations:

   a. Find remainder R of K divided by J.

   b. If R is zero, then

      (1) put out J.

      (2) Stop.

   Otherwise,

      (1) save J in K.

      (2) Save R in J.

A hand simulation, called a *trace*, is performed by tracing through the algorithm for some trial information with known results.

The simplest way to do this is to make a table of identifiers (names), keeping a record step by step of what is saved in each identifier during each pass. (When the steps in the repeated group are being performed the first time, this is known as the *first pass*. The second execution of the group is known as the *second pass*, and so on.) A trace of Euclid's algorithm for the numbers 36 and 88 is shown in Figure 2-9.

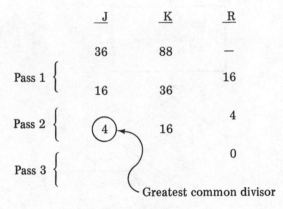

Figure 2-9.   Trace of Euclid's algorithm for the numbers 36 and 88.

A trace of the algorithm for finding the largest number for the case in which the numbers on the cards are 7, 5, 8, 12, 4, and 2 is shown in Figure 2-10. Figure 2-11 is the solution diagram with the refinement of using names, and Figure 2-12 is the corresponding flowchart.

EXERCISES

1. Construct a computer solution diagram for finding the smallest number of a set of numbers, each of which appears on one computer card.

2. Construct a flowchart for exercise 1.

3. Construct a computer solution diagram for an algorithm that finds both the smallest and largest numbers of a set of numbers, each of which appears on a computer card.

	N	MAX
	7	7
Pass 1	5	
Pass 2	8	8
Pass 3	12	(12)
Pass 4	4	
Pass 5	2	
Pass 6	(blank)	

largest number

Figure 2-10. Trace of algorithm for finding the largest number of the numbers 7, 5, 8, 12, 4, and 2.

Given	*Transformations*	*Required*

Stack of cards with number on each card.	1. Read N from first card.
	
	2. Save N in MAX.
	
	3. Repeat the following steps:
	  a. Read N from next card.
	  b. If card is blank, then
	    (1) write MAX.
	    (2) Stop.
	  Otherwise
	    (1) compare N with MAX.
	    (2) If N is larger, then save N in MAX.
		Largest number.

Figure 2-11. Computer algorithm for finding the largest number.

4. Construct a flowchart for exercise 3.

5. Perform a trace on the algorithm in exercise 1 for the numbers 7, 5, 8, 12, 4, and 2.

6. Perform a trace on the algorithm in exercise 3 for the numbers 7, 5, 8, 12, 4, and 2.

7. Perform a trace on Euclid's algorithm (computer solution) for the numbers 45 and 235.

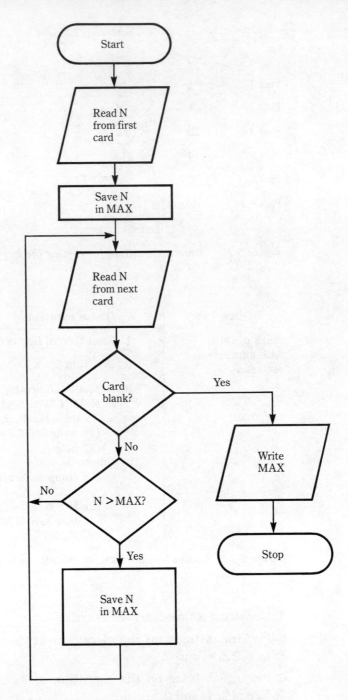

Figure 2-12.   Flowchart for finding the largest number.

8. Perform a trace on Euclid's algorithm (computer solution) for the numbers 416 and 822.

9. Construct a computer solution diagram for printing a list of all odd numbers contained in a set of numbers, each of which appears on a computer card.

10. Perform a trace on the algorithm in exercise 9 for the numbers 12, 7, 8, 2, 9, and 1.

11. Construct a computer solution diagram for counting the ages in the range 18–22, inclusive, as they are read on computer cards.

12. Perform a trace for the algorithm in exercise 11 for the ages 65, 18, 32, 23, 46, 2, and 20.

13. Construct a computer solution diagram that finds all of the even numbers in a set of ten numbers.

14. Construct a computer solution diagram that finds and prints all two-digit odd numbers that are not divisible by 3 in a set of 100 numbers.

15. Suppose that a savings account earns 10% interest daily and that it is compounded daily. One dollar is deposited into the account each day. Construct a computer solution diagram that prints the daily balance of the account for 365 days.

16. Construct a computer solution diagram that counts the number of times that the number 7 occurs in a set of 100 numbers.

17. Suppose that Mr. Rich deposits $10,000 into a savings account that earns 5% interest annually and that Mr. Thrift deposits $5,000 into a savings account that earns 15% interest annually. Construct a computer solution diagram that finds and prints the annual balances until Mr. Thrift's balance exceeds Mr. Rich's. Assume that no other deposits are made.

18. Construct a computer solution diagram that prepares separate lists of names of males and females from a list containing names and sex.

19. Construct a computer solution diagram for the following problem. Given a list of names and ages, prepare a list of names of people aged 65 and over.

20. Construct a computer solution diagram for the following problem. Given a list of names with ages and states of residence, prepare a list of names of people aged 65 and over who live in Arkansas and Oklahoma.

3
READING, WRITING, AND ARITHMETIC

It is shocking to find how many people do not believe they can learn, and how many more believe learning to be difficult. Muad'Dib knew that every experience carries its lesson.

Frank Herbert
Dune

All programmers are optimists. Perhaps this modern sorcery especially attracts those who believe in happy endings and fairy godmothers.

Frederick P. Brooks, Jr.
The Mythical Man-Month

Chapters 1 and 2 have provided a foundation upon which we can build. Now it is time to lay some bricks; it is time to begin solving computer-oriented problems.

When solving a problem, we develop a set of systematic and ordered transformations, a *process*, for transforming the initial situation into the required situation. To use the computer to perform processes, we must state the transformations in well-known computer operations.

PROGRAMMING LANGUAGES
AND PSEUDOCODE

Many programming languages are available for the programmer. A few of them are Fortran (Formula Translation), COBOL (Common Business Oriented Language), BASIC (Beginner's All-purpose Symbolic Instruction Code), and Pascal and PL/1 (both general purpose languages).

We shall make extensive use of *pseudocode*. Pseudocode is English that has been structured and abbreviated to allow the programmer to state well-known computer operations clearly and concisely by following certain conventions. Pseudocode helps programmers by freeing them from the complication of coding in a specific language, so that they can concentrate on the problem-solving process. (*Pseudo* means "false" or "pretended." Thus, we shall use a "pretended" computer code for constructing programs before translating them into a specific programming language later.)

Five computer operations were presented in the last chapter. Now we shall focus on three of them and develop their pseudocode:

Perform arithmetic (add, subtract, multiply, divide).

Receive and put out information.

Save a piece of information for later use.

SAVING INFORMATION

Information is saved, or stored, in a computer in a place called the *memory*, or *storage*. The memory is divided into units, each uniquely identified by an address.

Post office boxes provide an analogy. Each box has its own number (address) so that it may be identified with no ambiguity. Each addressable box is used to store information (mail). Though the box and its address never change, its contents change frequently. The box may contain a letter, a magazine, or a bill. (An important distinction between a mailbox and a unit of memory is that a mailbox may contain many items at one time, whereas a unit of memory may contain only one item at a time.) In summary, a post office box is a unique location for the temporary storage of information.

The unit of memory (hereafter referred to as *storage location* or *memory location*) is also a unique location for the temporary storage of information. At one instant a memory location may contain the price of gold; in the next it may contain the word *tree* or any other piece of information that will "fit" into it. (What will fit into a specific location varies from computer to computer and is beyond the scope of the present discussion.)

In programming, storage locations are identified by unique *names*, and each name corresponds to an address. These names are chosen to describe in some manner the information stored. A storage location used to store an employee's hourly wage might be called WAGE; the amount of a sale could be called AMOUNT or SALE; a student identification number might be STDNTID or STUDENT-ID-NUMBER.

The name simply refers to (or addresses) a particular storage location. Its contents are placed in it temporarily for later use, just as mail is placed temporarily in a post office box.

Each programming language has rules for constructing names. In pseudocode, however, we use convenient and appropriate English. For names we have two options: a description of the information or the actual name, written in uppercase letters so that we can distinguish it from a description. For example, a memory location to contain an employee's name may be designated NAME or *employee name*. We might refer to the former as its formal name, the latter as its descriptive name. Names must be natural, clear, and unambiguous.

A computer programmer can place information into a storage location by means of an *assignment statement*. The assignment statement instructs the computer to place a specified piece of information into a specified storage location. In pseudocode one could say, "Assign the employee number to EMPNUM" or "Save the employee number in EMPNUM." If the piece of information to be saved results from a calculation, one could say, "Compute AREA" or "Calculate the interest INT." The two latter examples are assignment statements in which the results are to be stored in the named locations. The assignment is implied but not explicitly stated. When a constant is to be stored, it may be convenient to say, "Set counter to zero" or "Initialize *pi* to 3.14159."

Assignment is usually accomplished in pseudocode by such key words as *set*, *initialize*, *save*, *store*, *compute*, and *calculate*; other key words are also possible. The assignment must be stated clearly, concisely, and unambiguously. It may be explicit (for example, *save*, *store*, *initialize*, or *set*) or implicit (for example, *compute* or *calculate*). Suppose a programmer wishes to place a zero (information) into a memory location that is to contain a counter. He or she could name the location COUNT, or simply refer to it descriptively as "counter." The following statements illustrate how this might be done in pseudocode:

Set counter to zero.

Set COUNT to zero.

Initialize counter to zero.

Store zero in counter.

If more than one counter is used in a problem, names such as COUNTER-1, COUNTER-2, and so on must be used to distinguish one counter from the next.

RECEIVING AND PUTTING OUT INFORMATION

When we enter information into a computer, we enter it in the form of characters that we can read, such as this printed page. Computers, however, cannot use information in this form; they translate it into a computer usable form. This is done through an *input device*, and the process is called *input*. Similarly, computers can translate their internal information into a form usable by humans through *output devices*, and this process is called *output*. We therefore use the terms *input* for receiving information and *output* for putting it out. Input and output together are referred to as *I/O*.

Input in pseudocode is usually indicated by the key words *read* and *get*. The statement "read two numbers, J and K" from Euclid's algorithm in Chapter 2 is an example of an input statement. This statement instructs the computer to use an input device to receive two numbers. The first is to be stored in memory location J, and the second in location K.

Input statements and assignments both store information in memory; how do they differ? Assignment moves "inside" information that is already in memory to another location in memory. Input, on the other hand, moves "outside" information into memory. After "outside" information has gone through the input process, it then becomes "inside" information and is available for the computer to use.

Output in pseudocode is usually indicated by the key words *print*, *write*, and *put* (or *put out*). The statement "put out J" from Euclid's algorithm in Chapter 2 instructs the computer to take the number stored in the location named J and, using an output device, move it "outside" in some readable form. Usually this is printed on paper or displayed on a screen.

Thus, input causes information outside the computer to be moved into memory; output causes information in memory to be moved outside the computer in some form usable by humans.

PUTTING OUT LABELS

Simply outputting the answers to problems is insufficient in most cases. A line of numbers representing such things as income, federal income tax, Social Security tax, and overtime would be meaningless without appropriate labels to indicate what the values mean. We must therefore label all output.

A label is a string of characters and is often called a *character string* or *literal*. We may use double or single quotes to enclose a literal. We can print a label in pseudocode by saying

Print 'label' or Print "label"

where *label* is an appropriate name, phrase, or sentence that identifies or describes the output. Anything placed between the quotes will be printed as it appears.

For example, if we have a value of 5 stored in memory at X, the two statements

Print 'X'.

Print X.

will produce output that looks like this:

X

5

If we wish to put the label on the same line with the value, we may say

Print 'X = ' and X.

This would produce the following:

X = 5

(Notice that two blanks are included in the literal: X blank equals blank.)

RECORDS

We speak of input and output in terms of units of information that we refer to as *records*. An *output record* usually means one line of printed output, and that will be its meaning in this book. An *input record* usually refers to one line of input (one card, if cards are being used, or a line of type if a terminal is being used), and that will be its meaning in this book.

ARITHMETIC

Computers are able to perform the four basic arithmetic operations: addition, subtraction, multiplication, and division. In pseudocode the name of the operation may be used—add, subtract, multiply, or divide—or the operation may be designated symbolically: + for addition, − for subtraction, * for multiplication, and / for division. Thus, one might say, "Add one to counter" or "Store counter + 1." Likewise, one could say, "Multiply price by tax rate" or "Compute price * tax rate."

We also symbolically represent exponentiation with two asterisks. For example, we write x^2 as X**2 in pseudocode.

In Chapter 1 the following algebraic expression was presented for converting degrees Fahrenheit (F) to degrees centigrade (C):

$$\frac{5(^\circ F - 32)}{9}$$

This expression could also be written (5*($^\circ$F — 32))/9. One might also say, "Subtract 32 from degrees F and multiply the result by 5; then divide by 9." All three ways of stating the calculation are acceptable in pseudocode, and there are others. You should use whichever seems best for you—provided it is clear, unambiguous, and correct.

IPO DIAGRAMS

In Chapters 1 and 2 we used diagrams for showing what is given and what is required and the transformations for going from what is given to what is required. Since given information must be input into the computer and required information must be output, from now on we shall use the column headings "Input" and "Output," instead of "Given" and "Required," respectively. These latter expressions are more appropriate within the context of computers. In Chapter 1 the set of transformations was referred to as a *process*. From now on we shall use the column heading "Process" instead of "Transformations." Diagrams with column headings "Input," "Process," and "Output" are called *IPO Diagrams*. In the "Input" column is placed a description of all information that must be available in order for the computer to perform the process. In the "Output" column is placed a description of all information that must be produced as the process is performed. The input information flows into the process, through the transformations in the process, and out of the process as the required output.

Let us go back to the diagram for Example 3 in Chapter 1 for the problem of converting degrees Fahrenheit to degrees centigrade. This time, however, the problem will be generalized so that any temperature expressed in degrees Fahrenheit can be converted to degrees centigrade.

Statement of problem: Construct a computer program that will convert any temperature expressed in degrees Fahrenheit to degrees centigrade. IPO Diagram 3-1 shows this.

IPO Diagram 3-1. Temperature Conversion

Input	Process	Output
Temperature in °F	1. Get temperature F. 2. Compute C: subtract 32 from F and multiply result by 5; then divide by 9. 3. Print C, ' deg C'. 4. Stop.	Temperature in °C

The IPO diagram contains the program in the "Process" column. Information required in the process is contained in the "Input" column. Required information that flows out of the process is contained in the "Output" column. The process is stated in pseudo-code, which is Englishlike, but uses key words to describe the process in terms of well-known computer operations. An important principle has been overlooked, however. The input temperature should also be included in the output for two reasons: first, because we must be certain that the computer received the input temperature correctly, we output the temperature to verify its correctness (this is called *echo checking*); second, the output is more meaningful if both temperatures are shown, degrees Fahrenheit and its equivalent degrees centigrade. Therefore, a better program is shown in IPO Diagram 3-2.

IPO Diagram 3-2. Temperature Conversion

Input	Process	Output
Temperature in °F	1. Get temperature F. 2. Print F, ' deg F'. 3. Compute C: subtract 32 from F and multiply result by 5; then divide by 9. 4. Print C, ' deg C'. 5. Stop.	Temperature in °F and equivalent temperature in °C

In IPO Diagram 3-2 the input temperature was put out immediately after it was input. It could also have been put out with the value of C, as in IPO Diagram 3-3.

IPO Diagram 3-3.   Temperature Conversion

Input	Process	Output
Temperature in °F	1. Get temperature F. 2. Compute C: subtract 32 from F and multiply result by 5; then divide by 9. 3. Print F, ' deg F' and C, ' deg C'. 4. Stop.	Temperature in °F and equivalent temperature in °C

Here is another example that illustrates the use of pseudocode for stating a program requiring input, output, saving, and arithmetic.

Statement of problem: Construct a program that will find the sum, difference, product, and quotient and remainder of any two numbers. IPO Diagram 3-4 illustrates this.

IPO Diagram 3-4.   Sum, Difference, Product, and Quotient and Remainder of Two Numbers

Input	Process	Output
Two numbers	1. Get two numbers, A and B. 2. Print 'A = ', A, 'B = ', B. 3. Compute SUM of A + B. 4. Compute DIFF of A — B. 5. Compute PROD of A * B. 6. Compute QUOT and REM of A / B. 7. Print 'SUM IS ', SUM. Print 'DIFFERENCE IS ', DIFF. Print 'PRODUCT IS ', PROD. Print 'QUOTIENT IS ', QUOT. Print 'REMAINDER IS ', REM. 8. Stop.	The input numbers and their sum, difference, product, and quotient and remainder

TRANSLATING A PSEUDOCODE PROGRAM INTO A COMPUTER PROGRAMMING LANGUAGE

Once the pseudocode program has been developed and tested for correctness, then and only then it is coded into some particular computer language. Since discussion of specific languages is beyond the scope of this book, you should refer to a textbook or manual describing the particular language with which you will be working. The following topics might be helpful:

Types of numeric data (integer or fixed-point and real or floating-point)

Numeric constants and variables

Arithmetic operators

Arithmetic expressions

Assignment statements (arithmetic)

Input and output (preferably unformatted or format free) of numbers and character strings (literals)

Basic units of a computer (memory, control, arithmetic/logical, and input/output)

EXERCISES

1. Construct an IPO diagram for the problem of computing the perimeter of a square with side s. Put out the values of the side and the perimeter. (Assume that s is positive.)
Construct a flowchart for the process.

2. Construct an IPO diagram for the problem of computing the perimeter of any rectangle. Put out the values of the length and width and the perimeter.
Construct a flowchart for the process.

3. The sum of the first n positive integers

$$1 + 2 + 3 + \ldots + n$$

is found by evaluating

$$\frac{n(n + 1)}{2}$$

Construct an IPO diagram for computing the sum of the first n integers. (For example, the sum of the first five integers ($n = 5$) is $1 + 2 + 3 + 4 + 5 = 15$. Evaluation of the algebraic expression for $n = 5$ also gives 15.) Print the value of n and the value of the sum.

Construct a flowchart for the process.

4. Perform a trace for the program in exercise 3 with n equal to 10. Notice how the input value 10 flows into and through the process, eventually producing the correct output value.

5. Construct an IPO diagram for the problem of finding a student's average test score for five tests. Print the student's name, five test scores, and the average score—all appropriately labeled.

Construct a flowchart for the process.

6. Perform a trace for the program in exercise 5 for Joe Sudds, who scored 76, 85, 92, 79, and 85.

7. The area of a triangle with sides a, b, and c units in length is

$$\sqrt{s(s-a)(s-b)(s-c)}$$

where

$$s = \tfrac{1}{2}(a + b + c)$$

Construct an IPO diagram for the problem of finding the area of a triangle with sides a, b, and c. Print with appropriate labeling the values of a, b, and c and the area.

Construct a flowchart for the process.

8. Perform a trace on the process in exercise 7 for the following values of a, b, and c, respectively: 3, 4, and 5.

9. Construct an IPO diagram for the following problem: Input the amount of deposit and the interest rate as a percentage. Print the old balance, the interest earned, and the new balance at the end of one year. Assume that the interest is computed once at the end of the year.

Construct a flowchart for the process.

10. Perform a trace for the problem in exercise 9 with a deposit of $2000 and an interest rate of 7.5%.

11. Construct an IPO diagram for the following problem: Input the high and low temperatures for a day. Print with descriptive headings the high, low, and average temperatures for the day.

12. Construct an IPO diagram for the following problem: Input a person's name, checking account number, checking account balance, and the amount of a check. Compute the new balance, and print with headings the name, account number, old balance, check amount, and new balance.

13. Construct an IPO diagram for the following problem: Input the amount of money spent to fill a gasoline tank, the price per gallon, and the number of miles driven since last filling the tank. Compute the miles per gallon, and print with headings the cost per gallon and the miles per gallon.

14. Construct an IPO diagram for the following problem: Compute the cost per mile using the input from exercise 13. Print with headings the number of miles driven and the cost per mile.

15. Construct a computer program in pseudocode that gets four numbers from a record, prints the numbers in reverse order, and prints the product of the second and fourth numbers and the sum of the first and third.

16. Construct a computer program in pseudocode that gets two numbers from a record and prints the numbers in the following sentences:

THE FIRST NUMBER IS xxxx.

THE SECOND NUMBER IS xxxx.

Notice that there are periods at the ends of the sentences. The number replaces xxxx.

17. Construct a computer program in psuedocode that gets a number N and prints the area of a square with side N and the area of a circle with radius N in the following form in which the correct values appear in place of *n* and *a*:

THE AREA OF A SQUARE WITH SIDE *n* IS *a*.

THE AREA OF A CIRCLE WITH RADIUS *n* IS *a*.

18. Construct a computer program in pseudocode that gets a person's name and prints the message

HELLO. IS YOUR NAME *name*?

in which the input name replaces *name*.

19. A record contains a first name, a middle name, and a last name. Construct a computer program in pseudocode that reads the three names and prints the last name followed by a comma and the first and middle names.

20. Construct a computer program in pseudocode that gets values for x and y, finds the value of the polynomial

$$4x^2 + 3xy - 9y^2$$

and prints the values of x, y, and the polynomial with descriptive labels. (The square of a number can be found by multiplying the number by itself or by using the exponentiation operator; thus, x^2 can be represented by $X*X$ or $X**2$.)

21. If we have the principal P at interest r compounded annually for n years, the amount A is given by the formula

$$A = P(1 + r)^n$$

Construct a computer program in pseudocode that gets the principal, the interest rate, and the number of years; computes the amount; and prints the principal, the interest rate, the number of years, and the amount—all with descriptive labels.

22. If we have the principal P at interest rate r compounded q times a year for n years, the amount A is given by the formula

$$A = P\left(1 + \frac{r}{q}\right)^{nq}$$

Construct a computer program in pseudocode that gets the principal, interest rate, times per year, and number of years and prints them along with the amount. All output must have descriptive labels.

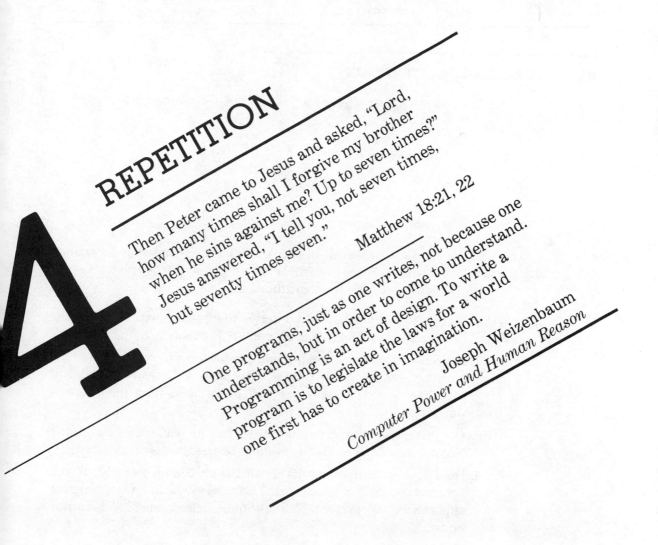

4 REPETITION

Then Peter came to Jesus and asked, "Lord, how many times shall I forgive my brother when he sins against me? Up to seven times?" Jesus answered, "I tell you, not seven times, but seventy times seven."

Matthew 18:21, 22

One programs, just as one writes, not because one understands, but in order to come to understand. Programming is an act of design. To write a program is to legislate the laws for a world one first has to create in imagination.

Joseph Weizenbaum
Computer Power and Human Reason

One of the greatest advantages of computers is that they are able to perform repetitious work and to do the same thing over and over without becoming tired, bored, or disgruntled. This capacity of *repetition* (also called *looping* and *iteration*) allows computers to perform a host of tasks. In this chapter we shall examine the concept of repetition and its corresponding pseudocode for stating the well-known computer operation given in Chapter 2:

Repeat any group of operations.

REPETITION, LOOPING, ITERATION

The following instructions are taken from a shampoo bottle:

> Wet hair.
>
> Apply shampoo.
>
> Lather.
>
> Rinse.
>
> Repeat application.

These instructions, which describe a process, are stated in operations well known to most people. Is this process an algorithm? Let us apply the four criteria for algorithms.

1. Is it sufficiently detailed to describe the transformations necessary to solve the problem (of shampooing)? Probably.

2. Is it unambiguous so that anyone can perform the transformations correctly every time? No. How many times is "repeat application" to be performed? We have no way of knowing from the information given.

3. Does it always give the same results for the same initial situation? Not necessarily, because the number of washings is unspecified.

4. Does it give correct results in all cases? Not necessarily. If the "correct result" is clean hair, how many times must "repeat application" be performed to produce "clean hair"? We do not know.

As it is stated, the process is therefore not an algorithm. If we followed the instructions literally, we would repeat them forever! This is known as an *infinite loop*. Within the loop no condition is stated for stopping. Can this process be altered so that it is an algorithm? Perhaps. Let us first consider methods of looping for computer applications and then return to the problem.

REPETITION GROUPS

The key words *loop*, *repeat*, *do*, and *perform* are commonly used to introduce a repetition group. The key words *end loop*, *end repeat*, *end do*, and *end perform*, respectively, are placed after the last operation in a repetition group to delineate clearly the bottom of the loop. We will use the key words *loop* and *end loop*.

We can control repetition within a computer program in several ways, including *loop with counter*, *loop while*, *loop until*, and a general loop that can be constructed in any computer language. *Loop with counter* is an important concept, and Chapter 7 is devoted to it. The general loop is an "unstructured" programming device used only when a programming language does not include one or more of the special constructs *loop while*, *loop until*, and *loop with counter*. We shall discuss the general loop briefly at the end of this chapter.

Loop while and *loop until* are similar constructs. We shall devote most of the chapter to the *loop while*, since it is more commonly used, and then briefly present the *loop until*.

THE *LOOP WHILE* CONSTRUCT

The general form of the *loop while* construct is shown in Figure 4-1. The condition in the *loop while* statement is some testable state, such as "A is equal to B," "X is greater than 1," and so on.

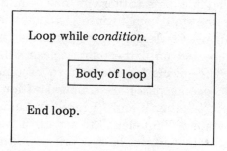

Figure 4-1.   The loop while construct.

The condition is tested at the top of the loop. Whenever the condition is *true*, the statement following the *loop while* is the next to be performed; that is, the loop is executed. If the condition is *false*, the loop is not executed, and the next statement to be performed is the one following the *end loop* statement.

The *end loop* statement, which is the final statement of a repetition group, functions to mark the end of the loop. If the loop is executed and processing reaches the *end loop*, the next statement to be performed is the *loop while*, thus completing a "pass" through the loop.

Between the *loop while* and the *end loop* lies a group of one or more statements that constitute the *body* of the loop, as shown in Figure 4-1. Within the body must be some means to change the condition to *false*, so that looping can be terminated.

To demonstrate these new terms, let us structure the shampooing instructions using the *loop while*.

> Wet hair.
>
> Loop while hair is not clean.
>
>> Apply shampoo.
>>
>> Lather.
>>
>> Rinse.
>
> End loop.

The body of the loop is made up of the statements "Apply shampoo," "Lather," and "Rinse." Notice that these are indented to set off the loop from the rest of the program, making it easier to read. The condition "hair is not clean" is found in the *loop while* statement and is *true* on the first pass (otherwise one would not be washing one's hair). After the statement "Rinse" is completed, the *end loop* is encountered; the next statement to be performed is the *loop while*. This process is repeated until the hair is clean when one arrives at the *loop while*. The means for the hair to become clean (that is, the condition to become *false*) are supplied within the body, since "Apply shampoo," "Lather," and "Rinse" presumably will change the hair from its state of "not clean" to a state of "clean." When this occurs, the next statement to be performed is the one following *end loop*. (There is none in this case, but it might be "Dry hair" if we were to expand the process.) The flowchart in Figure 4-2 will help you to visualize this procedure.

In summary, the *loop while* contains

1. a *loop while* statement that has some testable condition for terminating the loop (tested at the top of the loop);

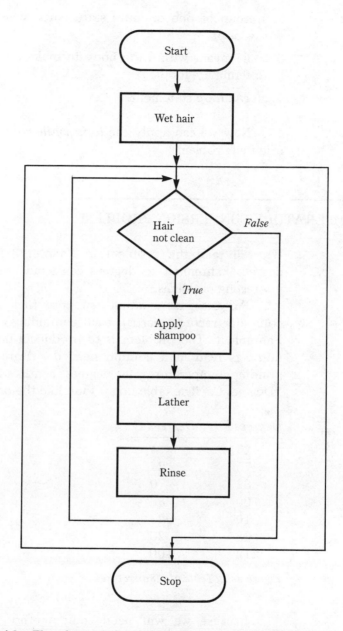

Figure 4-2. Flowchart of the shampooing process using loop while. The repetition group is enclosed within a large box. Notice that the test is at the top of the loop.

2. a group of one or more statements, which is called the *body* of the loop;

3. some means within the body to make the condition *false* (that is, to terminate looping);

4. an *end loop* statement.

Now we can apply the *loop while* construct to some computer-oriented problems.

THE TEMPERATURE CONVERSION PROBLEM

We will take the problem in Chapter 3 involving conversion of degrees Fahrenheit to degrees centigrade and expand it into more interesting problems.

For the first example, suppose that we are given a stack of computer records (cards), each containing a temperature in degrees Fahrenheit. The problem is to produce a printed table showing the numbers read in a column headed "Degrees F" and their corresponding temperatures in degrees centigrade in a column headed "Degrees C." The table might look like the one in Figure 4-3.

Degrees F	Degrees C
25	−4
75	24
32	0
100	38
−10	−23
68	20
212	100

Figure 4-3.   Table of temperatures.

Because we will need some method to determine when to terminate the looping, we will place a *trailer record* containing 999 at the end of the stack. A *trailer record* is a record containing some datum that will be clearly recognizable from data to be processed. Since 999 is an unlikely temperature, it is suitable for this loop. If the records were to contain a set of test scores, a trailer record containing —1 or any other negative number could be used. The condition for our loop will be one of the following:

Loop while temperature F is less than 999.

Loop while temperature F does not equal 999.

Either would be suitable.

When constructing a *loop while* repetition group, we must keep in mind that the test is at the top of the loop. This means that we have to "initialize," or set a value to, the condition. In this case it means reading the first record before entering the loop. If we do not read the first record before entering the loop, we have no Fahrenheit temperature to test in the *loop while* statement.

The next record must be read at the bottom of the loop upon completion of the first pass through the loop. We must get the next temperature value in preparation for the test that will occur at the top of the loop when it is repeated. Each subsequent record will be read at the bottom of the loop.

An IPO diagram with a pseudocode program that will produce the required output can be easily constructed, as in IPO Diagram 4-1. The flowchart is shown in Figure 4-4.

The next example prints a conversion table starting at 0° F and ending with 100° F in one-degree intervals. There will be no input for

IPO Diagram 4-1. Temperature Conversion Table

Input	Process	Output
A stack of records (cards), each with a temperature in degrees F. Trailer record with 999.	1. Print column headings: 'Degrees F' and 'Degrees C'. 2. Read temperature F. 3. Loop while F is not 999. Compute C. Print F and C. Read next F. End loop. 4. Stop.	Table of temperatures with headings, showing degrees F and degrees C.

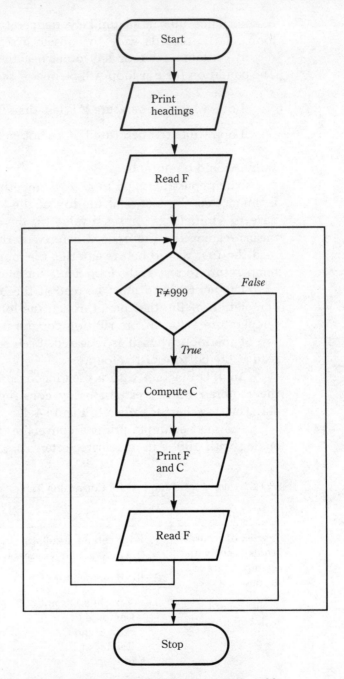

Figure 4-4.   Flowchart for the temperature conversion table.

this process, as shown in IPO Diagram 4-2. Notice that we must still initialize F.

IPO Diagram 4-2. Temperature Conversion Table in One-Degree Increments

Input	Process	Output
None.	1. Print column headings: 'Degrees F' and 'Degrees C'. 2. Set F to zero. 3. Loop while F is less than or equal to 100. 　Compute C. 　Print F and C. 　Add 1 to F. End loop. 4. Stop.	Table of temperatures, showing degrees F and degrees C, in one-degree increments from $0°$ F to $100°$ F.

EUCLID'S ALGORITHM

To use the *loop while* for Euclid's algorithm (see Chapter 2), the value of R must be computed before entering the loop. The computation of the next value of R must be placed at the bottom of the loop. One must be careful to notice these types of requirements when using the *loop while*. IPO Diagram 4-3 shows Euclid's algorithm using the *loop while*. The flowchart is shown in Figure 4-5.

THE *LOOP UNTIL* CONSTRUCT

As we have noted, the *loop until* is similar to the *loop while*. One difference is that in the *loop while* the test is at the top, but in the *loop until* the test is at the bottom. (The COBOL language is an exception. Its PERFORM UNTIL loop has the test at the top.) Since the test is at the bottom, the body of the loop is always performed at least once. Even though the test condition is initially *false*, that will not be discovered until one pass through the loop is completed.

The other chief difference is that the logic of the *loop until* statement is the opposite of the *loop while*. Where we said, "Loop while F *is not* 999" before, with the *loop until* we would have to say, "Loop until F *is* 999."

IPO Diagram 4-3.   Euclid's Algorithm with *Loop While*

Input	Process	Output

Two numbers, smaller followed by larger.	1. Read two numbers, J (smaller) and K (larger).
	
	2. Print 'The numbers are ', J, ' and ', K.
	
	3. Compute remainder R of J/K.
	
	4. Loop while R is not zero.
	   Save J in K.
	   Save R in J.
	   Compute new R of J/K.
	   End loop.
	
	5. Print 'Greatest common divisor is ', J.
	
	6. Stop.
		Greatest common divisor.

Now let us use the *loop until* in the temperature conversion problem to produce the table in Figure 4-3.

THE TEMPERATURE CONVERSION PROBLEM WITH *LOOP UNTIL*

The temperature conversion program in IPO Diagram 4-1 can be structured using the *loop until* construct. The new program is shown in IPO Diagram 4-4. The flowchart appears in Figure 4-6. Notice in the flowchart that the test is at the bottom of the loop.

IPO Diagram 4-4.   Temperature Conversion Table Using *Loop Until*

Input	Process	Output

A stack of records (cards), each with a temperature in degrees F.
 	
Trailer record with 999.
	1. Print column headings: 'Degrees F' and 'Degrees C'.
	
	2. Read temperature F.
	
	3. Loop until F is 999.
	   Compute C.
	   Print F and C.
	   Read next F.
	   End loop.
	
	4. Stop.
		Table of temperatures with headings, showing degrees F and degrees C.

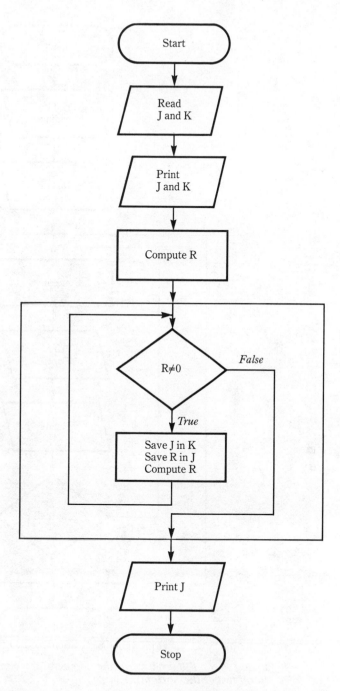

Figure 4-5.   Flowchart for Euclid's algorithm using the **loop while.**

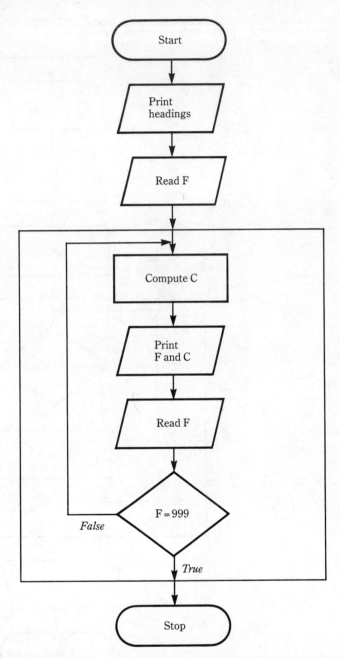

Figure 4-6. Flowchart for the temperature conversion table using loop until
(loop test at the bottom).

There is a problem with the process in IPO Diagram 4-4. What happens if the first record is the trailer record? Perform a trace on the process and determine what the problem is. (Recall that the body of a *loop until* is always performed at least once.)

THE GENERAL LOOP

A general loop in pseudocode appears in Figure 4-7. The loop test may be located anywhere in the loop. The body of the loop is indented so that it stands out clearly. The test statement is not indented, however, so that it will stand out clearly from the statements in the body.

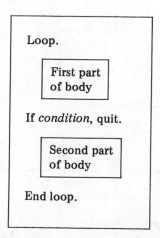

Figure 4-7.   *A general loop in pseudocode.*

When the test condition is *true*, looping is terminated by "quit." "Quit" means that the statement following *end loop* will be performed next.

A flowchart illustrating the general loop appears in Figure 4-8. Recall that the test may occur anywhere in the loop. Part 1 of the body may be *null* (that is, it may contain no statements), which places the test at the top of the loop. Similarly, the second part of the body may be null, which places the test at the bottom.

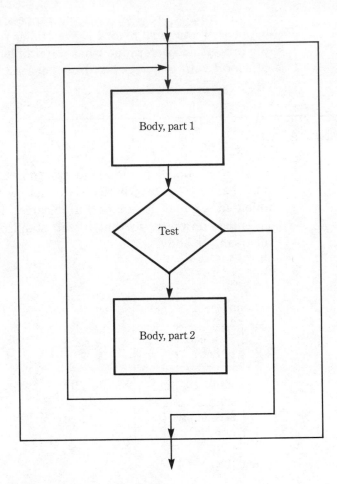

Figure 4-8.   Flowchart for the general loop.

The general loop is used when the *loop while* or *loop until* is not available in the computer programming language that one is using.

TRANSLATING A REPETITION GROUP
INTO A COMPUTER LANGUAGE

Some computer languages have no statements that allow direct translation from pseudocode. This is the case for two popular languages: standard BASIC and ANSI Fortran. In those cases in which the constructs are not available, the general loop must be used. Refer to Appendix I for Fortran and to Appendix II for BASIC.

Most computer languages provide statements for repetition that allow direct translation from pseudocode. Pascal is a good example. Appendix III shows the statements in Pascal that correspond to pseudocode constructs for repetition.

EXERCISES

1. Construct a flowchart for the pseudocode program in IPO Diagram 4-2.

2. In exercise 2 of Chapter 3 you were to construct an IPO diagram for finding the perimeter of any rectangle. Expand this so that a table of sides and perimeters is printed. Assume that each record contains two sides, S1 and S2, and that the trailer record contains an S1 of zero. Do this in both *loop while* and *loop until*, and design appropriate flowcharts.

3. Referring to the second temperature conversion example in this chapter (IPO Diagram 4-2), construct an IPO diagram that produces a similar table. In this case, however, read the starting and final temperatures and the number of degrees to increment from an input record (in that order). This makes the program more general so that it can produce a table covering essentially any range of temperatures.

4. Perform a trace for exercise 3 using your own set of input data.

5. Perform a trace for IPO Diagram 4-3 (Euclid's algorithm) for the numbers 45 and 235 to verify that the loop is properly constructed.

6. Perform a trace for the process in IPO Diagram 4-4 using 212, −40, 32, and 999. (You may need to refer to IPO Diagram 3-1 for computing C.)

7. Suppose that in a particular problem the test condition for terminating looping could be satisfied before the loop is entered—in which case the body of the loop is never performed. Which loop construct would you use to accomplish this? Why?

8. The Fibonacci sequence is defined to be

1, 1, 2, 3, 5, 8, 13, 21, . . .

The first two numbers are 1, and each subsequent number is found by adding the two previous numbers. In other words, the third number is found by adding the first to the second, the fourth is the sum of the second and third, and so on. Construct an IPO diagram that prints the elements of the Fibonacci sequence up to 377.

9. Construct a flowchart for exercise 8 and trace the program.

10. Given a set of inventory records—each containing the name of an item, the quantity sold this year, and the quantity sold last year—construct an IPO diagram that produces an inventory list showing the increase or decrease of the quantity sold for each item. Use a blank trailer record.
  Construct a flowchart.

11. Given a set of inventory records—each containing the stock number, item name, unit price, quantity on hand, and quantity sold—construct an IPO diagram that produces an inventory list in tabular form with a title and column headings. Each line of the table contains all of the input information for each item plus the value of the items on hand (unit price times quantity on hand), the value of the items sold (unit price times quantity sold), and the total value of items on hand and items sold. Use a blank trailer record.

12. Construct an IPO diagram for the following problem: Each record of a set of records contains a person's name, address, and city and state. Print a table with title and column headings containing the names and addresses and line numbers. The trailer record is blank. A sample output is shown as follows.

```
                     LIST OF RESIDENTS


       NAME                ADDRESS              CITY/STATE

1. TIM TEDERLY        P.O. BOX X23       HOUSE SPRINGS, MO

2. TINA TIMBERLANE    437 POSSOM TROT    MANFORD,  TN

3. TULA  PEMBERLY     STAR ROUTE         MANITEE, MN
```

You must use a counter for producing the line numbers.

13. Construct an IPO diagram for the following problem: The first record of a set of records contains a bank account number and a balance. Each of the remaining records contains the amount of

a check. The trailer record contains zero. Construct an IPO diagram that prints the account number and starting balance, lists the amounts of the checks, and prints the final balance. All output must be clearly labeled.

14. Construct an IPO diagram for the following problem: Given a set of records—each containing a number—compute and print the average of the numbers. The trailer record contains the number −999. You must use a counter to count the numbers.

15. Construct an IPO diagram for the following problem. Given a set of records—each containing two numbers—compute and print the average of the first numbers on the records, the average of the second numbers, and the average of all of the numbers. The first number is −999 on the trailer record. You must use a counter to count the number of records.

16. A savings account earns 10% daily interest compounded daily. One dollar is deposited into the account each day. Construct an IPO diagram that prints the number of the day and the daily balance until it exceeds $500. You must use a counter to produce the number of the day.

17. A person borrows $5000 from a bank at 1% interest per month. He or she makes monthly payments of $200 on the loan. Construct a computer program in pseudocode that prints the monthly balance until the loan is paid off—that is, until the monthly payment is equal to or exceeds the balance. (Interest is found by multiplying the balance by the interest rate. The new balance is found by adding the old balance and the interest and subtracting the payment.)

18. The daily fine for an overdue library book is 10¢ for the first day and increases by 1¢ for each succeeding day—that is, 11¢ for the second day, 12¢ for the third day, and so on. The total fine is the sum of the daily fines. Construct a computer program in pseudocode that gets the number of days that a book is overdue, and prints with descriptive labels the number of days and the total fine. You must use a counter for the days.

19. Construct a computer program in pseudocode that prints a sequence of 15 numbers. The first number is 1, the second 2, the third 4, and so on; each number is twice the preceding number.

20. Construct a computer program in pseudocode that prints the

sequence of numbers described in exercise 19, except that the sequence is continued until the next number exceeds 100,000.

21. In exercise 9 of Chapter 3, the new balance is computed at the end of one year. Modify the problem so that it prints the year, the old balance, the interest earned, and the new balance at the end of each year for ten years. You must use a counter for the year. Print the output in tabular form with column headings.

22. Modify the problem in exercise 21 so that the program prints the table for as many years as it takes for the new balance to equal or exceed three times the original deposit.

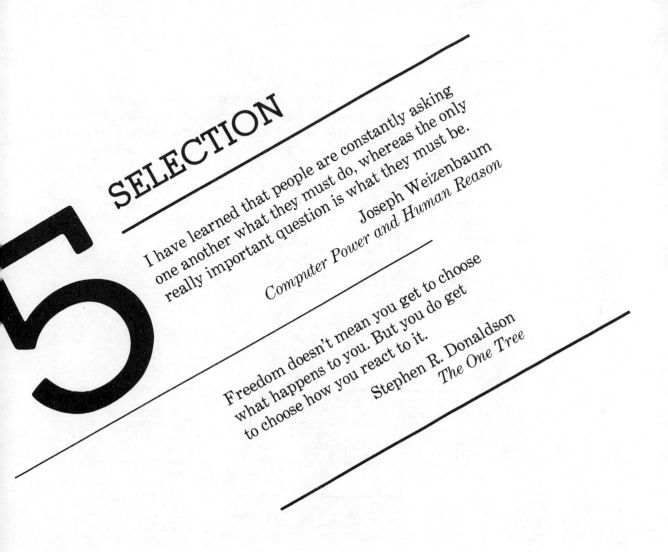

5 SELECTION

I have learned that people are constantly asking one another what they must do, whereas the only really important question is what they must be.

Joseph Weizenbaum
Computer Power and Human Reason

Freedom doesn't mean you get to choose what happens to you. But you do get to choose how you react to it.

Stephen R. Donaldson
The One Tree

Selection is perhaps the most powerful well-known computer operation. Selection is the name for operation 2 from Chapter 2: compare two pieces of information and select one of two alternative actions, depending on the outcome of the comparison. It allows the computer to alter the path of the program, depending on the circumstances.

THE STRUCTURE OF A SELECTION GROUP

A selection group consists of a test and two sets of one or more operations (statements). The test must be stated so that it yields a *true* or *false* result. One set of statements is performed when the outcome of the test is *true*. The other set is performed when the result is *false*. The flowchart in Figure 5-1 illustrates the *flow of control* through a selection group. The two sets of statements are mutually exclusive; that is, only one is performed. The next statement to be performed is then the statement following the selection group.

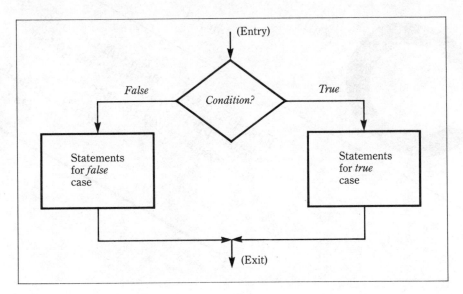

Figure 5-1.   Flowchart of the general form of the selection group.

There is a special case of the selection group in which the *false* case is null, or contains no statements. This type of selection group is illustrated in Figure 5-2.

The only difference between these two types of selection groups is that if the *false* case is null, a *false* result simply causes an exit from the selection group and no statements are executed.

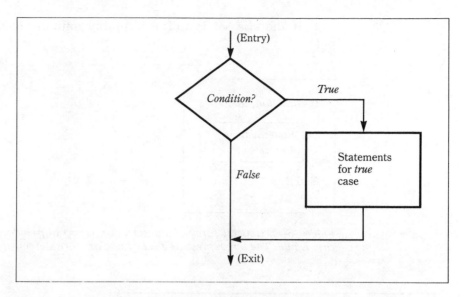

Figure 5-2.   Flowchart of a selection group having a null false case.

PSEUDOCODE FOR THE SELECTION GROUP

The key words *if*, *then*, and *else* are used for selection. *End if* is placed at the end (bottom) of the selection group. The general structure is shown in Figure 5-3. It is very important that the statements in the *then* and *else* sets be indented under their corresponding key words so that each stands out clearly from the other.

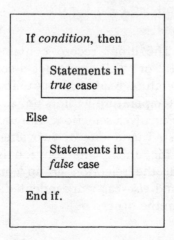

Figure 5-3.   General form of the selection group in pseudocode. The boxes represent sets of one or more statements.

If the *else* set is null, it is simply omitted, as shown in Figure 5-4.

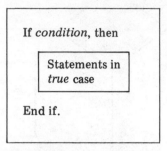

If *condition*, then

> Statements in *true* case

End if.

Figure 5-4. General form of the selection group in pseudocode when the else *case is null. The box represents a set of one or more statements.*

EXPANDED TEMPERATURE CONVERSION PROBLEM

We have used the temperature conversion problem for illustrating arithmetic and looping. Degrees Fahrenheit were converted into degrees centigrade. Now consider the problem of converting either from degrees Fahrenheit to degrees centigrade or from degrees centigrade to degrees Fahrenheit. The formulas for conversion are

$$\deg C = \frac{5(F - 32)}{9} \text{ and } \deg F = \frac{9}{5}C + 32$$

Statement of problem: The input record contains a temperature followed by its units, "F" or "C." Construct a computer program that will print the temperature read, with its units, from the input record and its equivalent temperature with its units.

The solution clearly involves selection. The units read from the input record must be tested, and one of two alternatives must be taken, depending upon the units. One solution is shown in IPO Diagram 5-1. Notice that the selection group corresponds to the general form. The *then* and *else* cases are indented; each stands out clearly and is distinct from the other.

IPO Diagram 5-1.   Temperature Conversion

Input	Process	Output
Temperature with units C or F.	1. Read temperature T and units U. 2. Print T and U. 3. If U is $'F'$, then compute C: $\dfrac{5(F-32)}{9}$. Print T, $'$ deg. F$'$ and C, $'$ deg. C$'$. Else compute F: $\dfrac{9}{5}C + 32$. Print T, $'$ deg. C$'$ and F, $'$ deg. F$'$. End if. 4. Stop.	Input temperature with units, and equivalent temperature with units. (C to F, or F to C.)

Figure 5-5 shows a flowchart for the temperature conversion problem.

THE LARGEST NUMBER PROBLEM

The largest number problem from Chapter 2 contains a selection group that has a null *else*. IPO Diagram 5-2 and the flowchart in Figure 5-6 illustrate this.

NESTED SELECTION GROUPS

Sometimes there may be a need to have a selection group within another selection group. Such a selection group is considered to be "layered" or "nested." There may be selection groups within both the *then* and the *else* cases, but often only one of the cases involves a nested selection. If only one of the alternative cases consists of

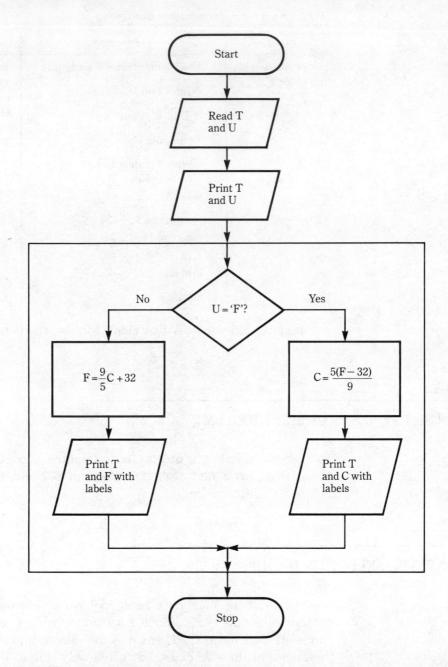

Figure 5-5. Flowchart for the temperature conversion problem. The selection group is enclosed within the large box.

IPO Diagram 5-2. The Largest Number

Input	Process	Output
Stack of records (cards) with number on each.	1. Read N from first record. 2. Print N. 3. Save N in MAX. 4. Read N from next record. 5. Loop while record is not blank. Print N. If N is greater than MAX, then save N in MAX. End if. Read N from next record End loop. 6. Print 'Largest number: ', MAX. 7. Stop.	Largest number.

a selection group, then the nested one should generally be associated with the *else* case.

Figure 5-7 illustrates the general form of the nested selection in which only the *else* case involves nesting.

Now let us look at an example that involves nested selection.

DOUBLE OVERTIME PROBLEM

Suppose we have an input record containing an employee name, the number of hours he or she worked during a one-week period, and the rate of pay. For every hour this person works over 40 hours, but less than or equal to 60 hours, per week, he or she is to be paid 1.5 times the regular pay; for every hour the employee works over 60 hours in one week, he or she is to be paid twice the regular pay. For example, an employee whose rate of pay is $5 and who works 65 hours in one week will receive $200 in regular pay (40 hours times $5), $150 in overtime pay (20 hours times $7.50), and $50 in double overtime pay (5 hours times $10) for a total of $400 for 65 hours of work.

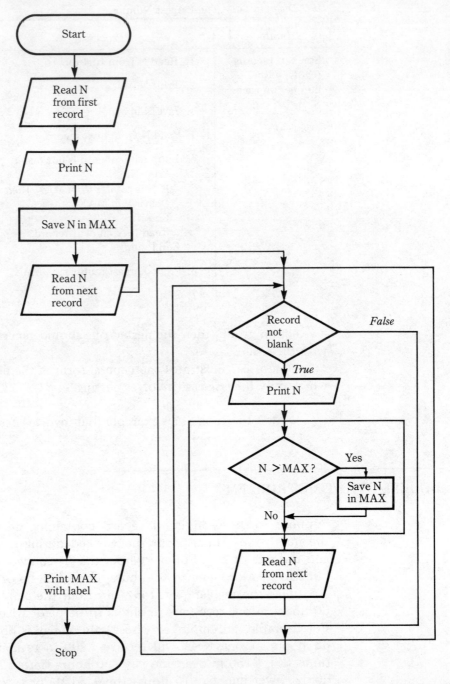

Figure 5-6. Flowchart for the largest number problem. The selection group is enclosed within the smaller box; the repetition group is enclosed within the larger box.

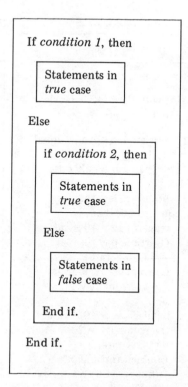

Figure 5-7. General form of a nested selection group. Notice that the nested selection group follows the same indentation rules of the "outer" or first selection group.

We want the program to read the input record; write the name of the employee, the hours worked, and the rate of pay; and then compute and write the total pay for the week. This program, which involves nested selections, is shown in IPO Diagram 5-3. The flow-chart appears in Figure 5-8.

TRANSLATING A SELECTION GROUP INTO A COMPUTER LANGUAGE

Most computer languages provide an IF/THEN/ELSE statement that allows direct translation from pseudocode. Pascal is a good example. Appendix III shows the IF statement in Pascal that corresponds to the *if-then-else* construct in pseudocode.

IPO Diagram 5-3. Double Overtime Problem

Input	Process	Output
Employee name. Hours worked. Pay rate.	1. Read name, hours, rate. 2. Print with descriptive labels name, hours, rate. 3. If hours are less than or equal to 40, then gross pay = hours $\times$ rate. Else if hours are less than or equal to 60, then regular pay = 40 $\times$ rate. Overtime pay = (hours $-$ 40) $\times$ (1.5 $\times$ rate). Gross pay = regular pay + overtime pay. Else regular pay = 40 $\times$ rate. Overtime pay = 20 $\times$ (1.5 $\times$ rate). Double overtime pay = (hours $-$ 60) $\times$ (2 $\times$ rate). Gross pay = regular pay + overtime pay + double overtime pay. End if. End if. 4. Print gross pay with label. 5. Stop.	Employee name. Hours worked. Pay rate. Gross pay. Descriptive labels.

Some computer languages have no statements that allow direct translation from pseudocode. This is the case for two popular languages: BASIC and ANSI Fortran, 1966 standard. The 1977 ANSI Fortran and some versions of BASIC include *if-then-else* constructs. In those cases in which the constructs are not available, selection must be contrived using what is available. Refer to Appendix I for Fortran 66 and to Appendix II for BASIC.

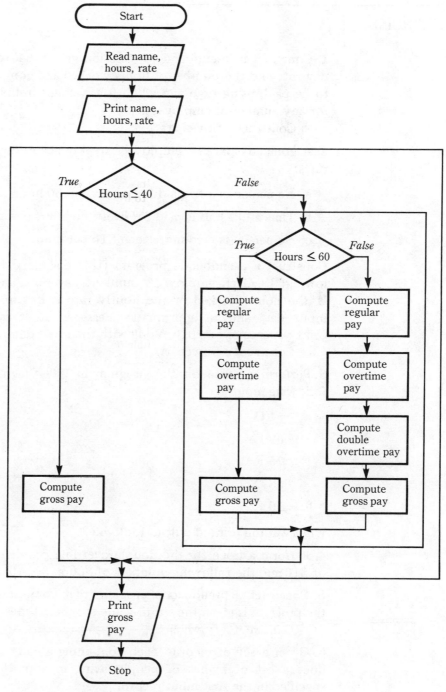

Figure 5-8.   Flowchart for the double overtime problem.

EXERCISES

1. Construct in pseudocode a selection group that receives an hourly pay rate and the number of hours worked and computes the amount to be paid, using time and a half for overtime hours (over 40 hours), for any number of employees.
   Construct a flowchart.

2. A company pays its employees weekly according to the following rules:

   a. No person can be paid for more than 60 hours.

   b. Time and a half is paid for overtime hours (over 40).

   c. No person is paid more than $15 per hour.

   Construct a pseudocode program (IPO diagram) that does the following: Read an employee's number, pay rate, and hours worked. If the hours worked or the hourly rate is out of range, print the input data and an appropriate message. Otherwise, compute and print the employee's pay, along with the input data, clearly labeled.
   Construct a flowchart.

3. Perform a trace on the program in IPO Diagram 5-1 using the following input:

   −4 C

   32 F

   75 F

   38 C

   −10 F

   What will the printed output look like?

4. Perform a trace for the double overtime problem using a pay rate of $10 and the following numbers of hours: 30, 40, 50, 60, 70.

5. Construct a pseudocode program that computes elapsed time if the program is given the starting and stopping times.
   Construct a flowchart.

6. Given a set of records, each containing a name and address, produce a list of names of people living in a particular city that is specified in the first input record.
   Construct a flowchart.

7. Construct a pseudocode program that prints the smallest and the largest numbers in a set of numbers.

Construct a flowchart.

8. You are given an input record containing a student's name and five test scores. The required output is the student's name and average score computed by summing the four highest test scores and dividing by four. (Discard the lowest test score.) Assign the letter grade as follows:

89.5–100 A

79.5–89.4 B

69.5–79.4 C

59.5–69.4 D

0–59.4 F

Construct a computer program in pseudocode that produces the required output.

9. You are given a record containing a customer's name, a purchase amount, and a tax code. The tax codes are defined as follows:

0 tax exempt (0%)

1 state sales tax only (3%)

2 state and local sales taxes (5%)

Produce a list containing name, purchase amount, sales tax, and total amount due for the customer.

10. In determining the appropriate insurance rate, an insurance company uses the following rules:

Female—standard rate times 0.85

Male over 25—standard rate

Other males—2 times standard rate

You are given a set of records, the first containing the standard rate and each of the remaining records containing a person's name and sex (M or F). There is a trailer record with X for the sex.

Construct a program (IPO diagram) that produces a list with headings of names and insurance rates.

11. A bank offers two types of checking accounts:

Type A:	Average Daily Balance	Monthly Service Charge
	$300.00 or more	None
	$200.00 — 299.99	$1.00
	$100.00 — 199.99	$2.00
	Less than $100.00	$3.00

Type B: $0.10 service charge for each check

You are given a record containing a person's name, average daily balance, and average number of checks written each month. Construct a computer solution in pseudocode that determines which type of checking account will be less expensive for that person, and print the person's name, the account type chosen, and the expected monthly service charge.

12. Suppose that you have taken a poll to determine some TV viewing habits. Each person polled was asked which network news program he or she watches most often. The information was compiled on a set of records—one per person—using the following codes:

    1 – ABZ
    2 – NBZ
    3 – YNN
    4 – ZBS
    5 – ZNN

Construct a computer solution in pseudocode to determine which network news program is watched by the most people.

13. Modify exercise 12 to present the results as percentages of viewers for each network as follows (data are hypothetical):

    35% watch ABZ.
    25% watch NBZ.
     5% watch YNN.
    27% watch ZBS.
     8% watch ZNN.

14. You are given a record containing a name, a checking account balance, an amount of a check, and a "flag." The flag will be one if the person has a line of credit with the bank, zero if the person does not. Construct a program in pseudocode that first determines whether the check amount is less than or equal to the balance. If so, print the message "Pay the check." If the check amount exceeds the account balance, determine whether the person has a line of credit. If so, print the message "Pay the check." If the person does not have a line of credit, print the message "Issue an overdraft notice."

15. Construct a computer program in pseudocode that does the following: Get the name and age of a first person and the name and age of a second person. Assume that the ages are different. Print the names and ages in the following form:

Name IS age YEARS OLD.

Determine which person is older, and print both names in the following form:

Name IS OLDER THAN name.

16. Modify the problem in exercise 15 so that the program can handle equal ages as well as unequal ages. In addition to the output described in exercise 15, for equal ages print the following:

Name IS THE SAME AGE AS name.

17. The cost of an ad is $1.00 for 15 or fewer words and $0.05 for each additional word. Construct a computer program in pseudocode that gets the number of words in an ad, computes the cost, and prints the number of words and the cost with identifying labels.

18. The cost of renting a particular tool is $4.50 for the first day, $3.00 a day for the next four days, and $6.00 a day thereafter. Construct a computer program in pseudocode that receives the number of days, computes the cost, and prints the number of days and the cost with identifying labels.

19. For a particular item in a store's inventory, the manager wants to keep at least a certain minimum number, but not more than a certain maximum. Construct a program in pseudocode that gets the name of the item, the maximum number, the minimum number, and the current inventory. If the current inventory is greater than the maximum, print the item name and by how many it exceeds the maximum in the following message:

Item name EXCEEDS MAXIMUM BY x UNITS.

If the current inventory has fallen below the minimum, print the name of the item and how many to order (maximum number minus current inventory) in the following message:

Item name IS BELOW MINIMUM. ORDER x UNITS.

If the current inventory is within the correct range but is within 5 of the minimum, print the name of the item and how many to order to bring the inventory up to the maximum (maximum number minus current inventory) in the following message:

Item name IS CLOSE TO MINIMUM. ORDER x UNITS.

Otherwise, print

INVENTORY FOR item name IS OK.

20. An income tax is computed by the following rules:

Annual Salary	Tax Rate
$0.00 – 9.999.99	No tax
$10,000.00 – 19,999.99	16%
$20,000.00 – 29,999.99	20%
$30,000.00 – 39,999.99	24%
$40,000.00 – up	26%

Construct a computer program in pseudocode that gets an annual salary, computes the income tax, and prints the salary and tax.

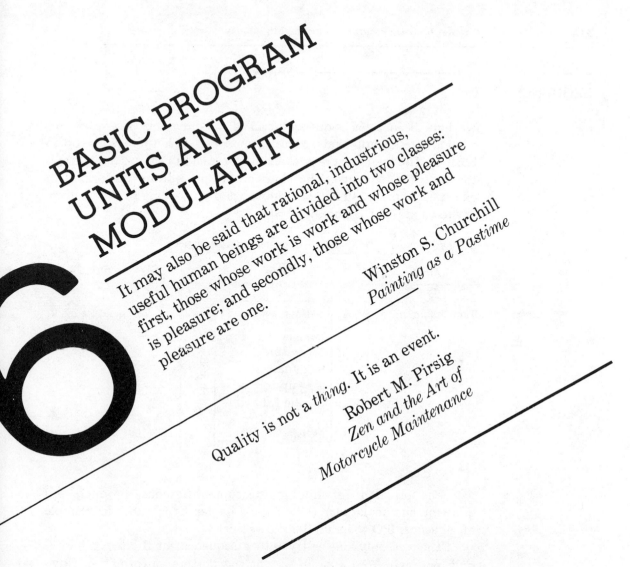

BASIC PROGRAM UNITS AND MODULARITY

It may also be said that rational, industrious, useful human beings are divided into two classes: first, those whose work is work and whose pleasure is pleasure; and secondly, those whose work and pleasure are one.

Winston S. Churchill
Painting as a Pastime

Quality is not a *thing*. It is an event.

Robert M. Pirsig
Zen and the Art of Motorcycle Maintenance

A *task* is a piece of work to be done, a result to accomplish, or a problem to solve. If a task is to be performed, a procedure, or process, must be available in order to complete the task. We have used IPO diagrams for stating processes. The process must also be correct for proper completion of the task. We have used the *trace* for verifying processes.

Processes stated in well-known computer operations can be broken down into groups of sequential steps (*sequences*), decisions with alternatives (*selections*), and/or repeated statements (*repetitions*). Computer programs are therefore constructed from three basic units: sequence, selection, and repetition.

SEQUENCE UNITS

We have been using sequence in all of our programs. A *sequence* is a set of statements that are performed one at a time from top to bottom. The temperature conversion program in Chapter 3 illustrates the use of a sequence. The steps of the process are performed or executed in order, starting at the top and proceeding to the bottom, as shown in IPO Diagram 6-1.

IPO Diagram 6-1.   Temperature Conversion (A Sequence)

Input	Process		Output
Temperature in °F.	1.	Get temperature F.	Temperature in °C.
	2.	Compute C: $\dfrac{5(F-32)}{9}$	
	3.	Print F, ' deg F', and C, ' deg C'.	
	4.	Stop.	

(Sequence)

The program for finding the sum, difference, product, and quotient and remainder (also from Chapter 3) is another example of sequence. IPO Diagram 6-2 shows this.

There is only one entry into a sequence: at the top. There is only one exit from a sequence: at the bottom. Information flows through a sequence: it enters at the top, usually undergoes transformations through the process, and exits at the bottom.

Each statement of a sequence can also be thought of as a sequence that has one entry and one exit. Information flows into and out of a statement and is altered by the operation(s) described in the statement. Just as we can "stack" statements to form a sequence, so we can stack sequences to form new sequences. Figure 6-1 shows a general structure of a sequence composed of smaller sequences. Each sequence has one entry and one exit, illustrated by the arrows.

Selection was discussed in detail in Chapter 5. Figure 6-2 shows the general form of selection units. Like sequence units, selection

IPO Diagram 6-2.   Add, Subtract, Multiply, and
Divide Two Numbers (A Sequence)

Input	*Process*	*Output*
Two numbers.	1. Get two numbers, A and B. 2. Print 'A = ', A, 'B = ', B. 3. Compute SUM of A + B. 4. Compute DIFF of A − B. 5. Compute PROD of A ∗ B. 6. Compute QUOT and REM of A / B. 7. Print 'SUM IS ', SUM. Print 'DIFFERENCE IS ', DIFF. Print 'PRODUCT IS ', PROD. Print 'QUOTIENT IS ', QUOT. Print 'REMAINDER IS ', REM. 8. Stop.	The input numbers and their sum, difference, product, and quotient and remainder.

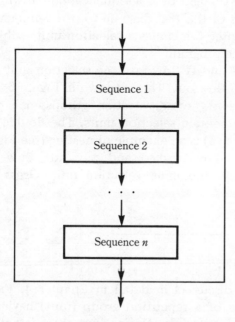

Figure 6-1.   A general form of a sequence consisting of a "stack" of n sequences.

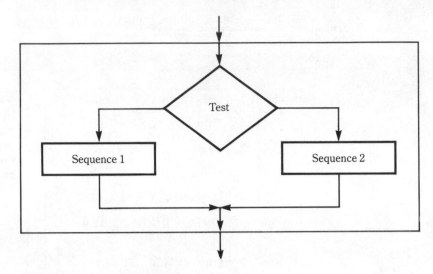

Figure 6-2.   General form of a selection unit.

units have one entry, at the top, and one exit, at the bottom. Information is processed the same way as in sequence units; it enters at the top and exits at the bottom. Each of the alternative paths of the selection may be thought of as a sequence, one of which may be null.

The process of the IPO diagram for the temperature conversion problem in Chapter 5 includes a selection unit within the sequence that makes up the program.

Values of T and U flow into the selection unit; values of T, U, and either F or C flow out. This is shown in Figure 6-3.

In the case of nested selection groups, one or both of the alternatives may contain selection units. The double overtime problem (from Chapter 5) is an example of nesting (see Figure 6-4).

Values of hours worked and pay rate flow into the outer selection unit and the inner selection unit. Gross pay flows out of both of them.

REPETITION UNITS

Repetition was discussed in detail in Chapter 4. Figure 6-5 shows the general form of a repetition group (unit) having the loop test at the top—the *loop while*. Notice that there is only one entry (at the top of the unit) and one exit (at the bottom).

1. Read temperature T and units U.

2. If U is $'F'$, then

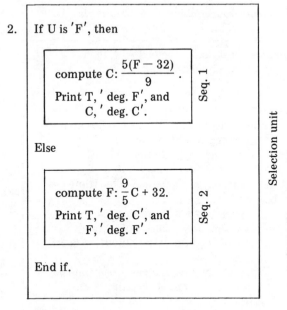

   compute C: $\dfrac{5(F-32)}{9}$.

   Print T, $'$ deg. F$'$, and
       C, $'$ deg. C$'$.

    Seq. 1

   Else

   compute F: $\dfrac{9}{5}C + 32$.

   Print T, $'$ deg. C$'$, and
       F, $'$ deg. F$'$.

    Seq. 2

   End if.

    Selection unit

3. Stop.

Figure 6-3.   A selection unit.

In the *process* portion of the IPO diagram for Euclid's algorithm (Chapter 4), the repetition unit is located in step 4 (see Figure 6-6).

The values of J, K, and R flow into the repetition unit, and the new values of J, K, and R flow out. We are interested only in the value of J, the greatest common divisor.

In the largest number problem (Chapter 5) the sequence within the repetition unit contains a selection unit. This is shown in Figure 6-7.

The second value of N and the value of MAX flow into the repetition unit, and the value of MAX flows out the bottom. The selection unit is within the body of the loop. Values of N and MAX (possibly a new value) flow out.

THE MODULAR STRUCTURE OF PROGRAMS

We have seen that programs are made up of sequence, selection, and repetition units. We have seen that a sequence may include

1.   Read name, hours, rate.

2.   Print name, hours, rate, with descriptive labels.

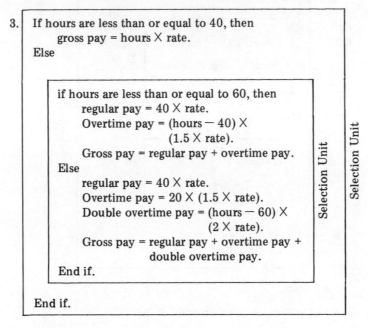

3.   If hours are less than or equal to 40, then
         gross pay = hours × rate.
     Else

         if hours are less than or equal to 60, then
                 regular pay = 40 × rate.
                 Overtime pay = (hours − 40) ×
                                 (1.5 × rate).
                 Gross pay = regular pay + overtime pay.
         Else
                 regular pay = 40 × rate.
                 Overtime pay = 20 × (1.5 × rate).
                 Double overtime pay = (hours − 60) ×
                                 (2 × rate).
                 Gross pay = regular pay + overtime pay +
                                 double overtime pay.
         End if.

     End if.

4.   Print gross pay with label.

5.   Stop.

Figure 6-4. An example of nested selection units.

repetition and/or selection units. Other combinations of sequence, selection, and repetition units are possible. In fact, any of the basic program units may include any type of unit and any combination of units. Stated simply, basic program units may be nested in any possible way.

Each basic program unit performs some simple task—that is, a *subtask* of a task that the entire program will perform. We have been thinking in terms of basic program units. Instead, let us begin to think in terms of simple subtasks. A subtask may require a single basic unit or some combination of units; either is referred to as a *module*. A module, being one or more basic units, has a single entry and a single exit. Information flows into it at the top and out of it at the bottom.

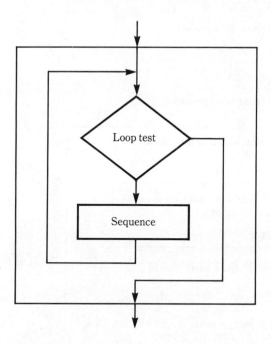

Figure 6-5. General form of a loop while *repetition unit (with test at the top).*

1.   Read two numbers, J (smaller) and K (larger).

2.   Print J and K with labels.

3.   Compute remainder R of K/J.

4.   Loop while R is not zero.
         Save J in K.
         Save R in J.
         Compute new R of K/J.
     End loop.
                                                    Repetition unit

5.   Print J with label.

6.   Stop.

Figure 6-6. Repetition unit from Euclid's algorithm.

1. Read N from first record.

2. Print N.

3. Save N in MAX.

4. Read N from next record.

5.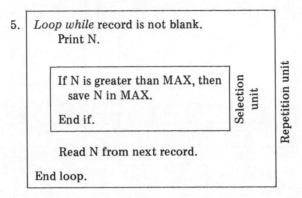

6. Print 'Largest number is ', MAX.

7. Stop.

Figure 6-7. Repetition unit, containing a (nested) selection unit, from the largest number algorithm.

We can divide any task into simple subtasks. Each subtask can be further divided into several subtasks. We can continue this subdivision until each subtask is simple enough so that we can easily construct its pseudocode.

This *modular* approach to programming makes the programming simpler, more systematic, and more likely to be free of errors. Since each module corresponds to a single subtask, the programmer has a much better chance of constructing a correct module than he or she does of correctly constructing an entire program without the modular approach. Furthermore, since each module has one entry and one exit, the programmer can more easily keep track of the flow of information through a program.

As modules are constructed and tested for correctness, they can then be "stacked" in the proper order. Generally, the information that flows into a module comes directly from the module that immediately precedes it. Likewise, the output of a module usually flows directly into the module that immediately follows it. (Some of the information that flows into a module may not be used; rather, it flows straight through. Information may also flow into a module from the "Input" column of the IPO diagram, or out of a module into the "Output" column.)

Modular structure provides an effective debugging tool. (*Debugging* is the process of identifying and removing errors, or *bugs*, in a program.) Because of the way information flows through a program, module by module, incorrect information flowing out of a module will affect the final results. By printing or displaying information as it comes out of each module (or in some cases, before it flows into a module, especially from the "Input" column), a module that contains an error can be quickly identified and corrected. (The debugging output statements can be removed from the program after it is verified.)

Modularity also aids in the problem-solving process. Since each task is composed of simpler subtasks, we can tackle the subtasks one at a time with relative ease. If a particular subtask proves to be too complicated, it can be further subdivided until it becomes manageable.

To illustrate the modular approach, we shall now examine a problem and its solution in detail.

A SAVINGS ACCOUNT PROBLEM

Suppose that a person deposits some money into a savings account. The interest is computed and added to the balance at the end of each year. The person would like to know what the balance would be at the end of some number of years at some particular rate of interest.

For example, suppose that the initial deposit is $200 and the interest rate is 10%. What is the balance at the end of five years? A table showing the year, the old balance, the interest earned, and the new balance at the end of each year appears in Figure 6-8.

INITIAL DEPOSIT $200
INTEREST RATE   10%
PERIOD   5 YEARS

YEAR	OLD BALANCE	INTEREST	NEW BALANCE
1	200.00	20.00	220.00
2	220.00	22.00	242.00
3	242.00	24.20	266.20
4	266.20	26.62	292.82
5	292.82	29.28	322.10

Figure 6-8.   A sample savings account report.

We want to be able to use any deposit, any interest rate, and any number of years. We also want a printed table like the one in Figure 6-8.

Let us begin the analysis of the problem by determining the required input and output, filling in the IPO diagram as we go. Since we are given a sample output in Figure 6-8, we know precisely what the required output is. Figure 6-9 shows the "Output" column of the IPO diagram.

Output

Deposit

Interest rate

Number of years

For each year:

year

old balance

interest

new balance

All with descriptive labels and headings

Figure 6-9.   The required output for the savings account problem.

What input must we use to produce the required output? Examination of the output quickly reveals the answer. Figure 6-10 shows the required input.

Input
_____

Amount deposited
Rate of interest
Number of years

Figure 6-10.   The required input for the savings account problem.

What steps or subtasks are required in the processing to transform the input into the output? Let us list some key subtasks without regard to order and detail. There is no uniquely correct way to do this. Different people will probably produce different lists. The point is to identify the major subtasks that must be performed.

Construct a list of major subtasks, and compare your list with the one in Figure 6-11.

Process
_____

Print a line of the table (year, old balance, interest, new balance).

Compute interest

Compute new balance.

Move new balance to old balance. (Notice that the new balance for a particular year becomes the old balance for the next year.)

Get the amount of deposit, interest rate, and number of years.

Print with descriptive labels the amount of deposit, interest rate, and number of years.

Print column headings.

Stop.

Figure 6-11.   Major subtasks in the process for the savings account problem. The subtasks are not necessarily in order, and details are deliberately omitted.

Have we identified all of the major subtasks? That question is not always easily answered, but the answer is probably yes for this relatively simple problem. However, as we add details later, we may find that we have omitted one or more major subtasks.

Now let us attempt to place the major subtasks of the process in order. Which subtask in Figure 6-11 must come first? Clearly, we cannot print values or perform computations with data that are not available. Therefore, getting the values of the deposit, the interest rate, and the number of years is probably the first subtask to perform.

After the deposit, interest rate, and number of years are available, they can be printed and used for computations. Which comes before the other—printing or computing? Examination of the output in Figure 6-8 gives the answer. We want the deposit, interest rate, and number of years printed before any computations are done.

What is next? We can see from Figure 6-8 that printing the table is next. The table consists of headings and the body of the table. The body consists of printed lines, each showing the year, old balance, interest, and new balance. Clearly, computations must precede printing a line of the table. Therefore, the order of these subtasks is: print headings, perform computations, and print a line of the table.

In what order do the computations occur? We must compute the interest before we can add it to the old balance to get the new balance.

Where does "Move new balance to old balance" fit into the ordered subtasks? It must occur after a line of the table is printed and before the next computation of interest occurs.

All of this ordering produces the process in Figure 6-12. The subtasks are numbered for convenience, since we will refer to them later.

Process

1. Get deposit, interest rate, and number of years.

2. Print with descriptive labels deposit, interest rate, and number of years.

3. Print column headings.

4. Compute interest.

5. Compute new balance.

6. Print a line of the table (year, old balance, interest, new balance).

7. Move new balance to old balance.

8. Stop.

Figure 6-12. Ordered major subtasks in the process for the savings account problem. Details are omitted.

(Did you become lost in the ordering procedure? It can happen easily. If so, read the material again, referring to Figures 6-8 and 6-12. Be sure that you see what is happening and that you are satisfied with Figure 6-12 before you go ahead.)

Now that we have identified the major subtasks and their order, we can begin to identify details for each major subtask.

It is useful at this point to identify any selection and repetition groups.

Are there any obvious selection groups in the process in Figure 6-12? (Are there any questions asked, tests performed, or conditions stated?) The answer is no.

Are there any repetition groups—that is, one or more major subtasks that are repeated? Yes, there is a group of repeated statements. The body of the table requires the repeated printing of a line. Computing the interest and the new balance must be repeated.

Now that we have identified the repetition group, or loop, let us determine which subtasks in Figure 6-12 belong in the loop.

Subtasks 1, 2, and 3 in Figure 6-12 are not repeated. Subtasks 4, 5, 6, and 7 are repeated and therefore belong in the loop. Subtask 8 is not repeated.

Now that we have identified the loop, we should be able to determine the structure of the loop. What determines when to quit looping? We want the looping to continue while the year is less than or equal to the number of years. Where does the year come from? We must have a year counter. That means that we must set it to its initial value (1) and add 1 to it each time a line is printed.

Now we must question whether we may have overlooked a major subtask. Should we have handled the year counter in the list of major subtasks? Some would say that it belongs with the major subtasks. Others would say that it belongs with the detailed subtasks. Recall that we said at the beginning of this discussion that different people would probably produce different lists of major subtasks. Whether by accident or design, we will include the year counter among the detailed subtasks.

Figure 6-13 shows the process with the loop in place.

We are now ready to proceed with detailing each major subtask, as necessary. Here we ask for each subtask, "Does this subtask need to be broken down into more detailed subtasks?" or "Is there sufficient detail so that we know exactly what to do?"

Process

---

1. Get deposit, interest rate, and number of years.

2. Print with descriptive labels deposit, interest rate, and number of years.

3. Print column headings.

4. Set year to 1.

5. Loop while year is less than or equal to number of years.

6.   Compute interest.

7.   Compute new balance.

8.   Print a line of the table (year, old balance, interest, new balance).

9.   Add 1 to year.

10.   Move new balance to old balance.

11. End loop.

12. Stop.

Figure 6-13. Ordered major subtasks in the process for the savings account problem, with the loop in place.

    Subtask 1: "Get deposit, interest rate, and number of years." This subtask is probably detailed enough.

    Subtask 2: "Print deposit, interest rate, and number of years, with descriptive labels." We could specify the labels in detail if we wish, but the output shown in Figure 6-8 provides necessary details.

    Subtask 3: "Print column headings." We could specify the headings and spacing in detail; however, as in subtask 2, reference to Figure 6-8 provides the necessary detail.

    Subtasks 4, 5, and 11 control the looping and are sufficiently detailed.

    Subtask 12: "Stop." There is nothing to add here.

    Only the body of the loop remains. Let us go through it one subtask at a time.

    Subtask 6: "Compute interest." The interest rate times the old balance gives the interest. The first time through the loop the old balance has not been assigned a value. Therefore, we must move the deposit into the old balance before looping begins. Furthermore, the interest rate is in the form of a percentage and must be divided by 100 before it can be used for computation. Therefore, we must divide the interest rate by 100 before looping begins. (We must move the deposit to the old balance and divide the interest rate by 100 only one time. These subtasks are not repeated and therefore are not in the loop.)

Subtask 4 now becomes three statements:

Move deposit to old balance.

Divide interest rate by 100.

Set year to 1.

Subtask 6 becomes

Compute interest by multiplying interest rate by old balance.

Subtask 7: "Compute new balance." The new balance is found by adding the old balance and the interest.

Subtask 8: "Print a line of the table (year, old balance, interest, and new balance)." We can refer to Figure 6-8 for necessary details.

Subtask 9: "Add 1 to year" and Subtask 10: "Move new balance to old balance" are both sufficiently detailed.

The more detailed process appears in Figure 6-14.

Once more we must go through the process subtask by subtask, asking whether more detail is necessary. Doing this, we find that the process is detailed enough.

IPO Diagram 6-3 contains the completed solution.

Perform a trace on the program using the input data in Figure 6-8 to verify that the program produces the required output in Figure 6-8.

We have gone through a detailed analysis of this problem to illustrate a procedure that one might use to develop the solution. There are many ways to approach the solution, and we have shown only one.

Next we will go through a more complex problem but in less detail. Rather we will summarize the development of a solution with brief discussion and IPO diagrams.

Process

1. Get deposit, interest rate, and number of years.

2. Print with descriptive labels deposit, interest rate, and number of years.

3. Print column headings.

4. Move deposit to old balance.

5. Divide interest rate by 100.

6. Set year to 1.

7. Loop while year is less than or equal to number of years.

8.   Compute interest by multiplying interest rate by old balance.

9.   Compute new balance by adding interest to old balance.

10.   Print a line of the table (year, old balance, interest, new balance).

11.   Add 1 to year.

12.   Move new balance to old balance.

13. End loop.

14. Stop.

Figure 6-14. Details of the process for the savings account problem.

THE REVOLVING CHARGE ACCOUNT PROBLEM

A company named TinyCorp is in the credit card business. For each customer the company keeps a record that shows the account number and the balance from the last report. If the account is overpaid (actually a negative balance), the amount of overpayment is followed by "CR." A balance of zero simply shows zero with no label attached. A balance due is followed by "DUE." Figure 6-15 shows a sample set of input records. Each record shows the account number, the amount of the transaction, and the type of transaction: purchase, refund, or payment. A finance charge of 2% of the balance

IPO Diagram 6-3.   Savings Account Problem

Input	Process	Output
Amount deposited.	Get deposit, interest rate, and number of years.	Deposit.
Rate of interest.		Interest rate.
Number of years.	Print deposit, interest rate, and number of years, with descriptive labels.	Number of years.
		For each year:
	Print column headings.	year
		old balance
	Move deposit to old balance.	interest
		new balance.
	Divide interest rate by 100.	
		All with descriptive labels and headings.
	Set year to 1.	
	Loop while year is less than or equal to number of years.	
	Compute interest by multiplying interest rate by old balance.	
	Compute new balance by adding interest to old balance.	
	Print a line of the table (year, old balance, interest, new balance).	
	Add 1 to year.	
	Move new balance to old balance.	
	End loop.	
	Stop.	

43-897-456	139.25	DUE
43-897-456	43.25	PURCHASE
43-897-456	30.00	PAYMENT
43-897-456	7.68	PURCHASE
43-897-456	28.97	REFUND
43-897-456	17.86	PURCHASE
(Blank trailer record)		

Figure 6-15.   A sample set of input records for the revolving charge account problem.

due from the last report is added to the unpaid balance before any transactions are processed. A report for each customer is prepared, showing the following information: account number, previous balance (with attached label, if required), finance charge (zero if not applicable), a list of transactions (amount and type), and the final balance (with attached label, if required). Figure 6-16 shows a sample report for one customer.

```
ACCOUNT NUMBER 43-897-456
PREVIOUS BALANCE        139.25  DUE
FINANCE CHARGE            2.79
    PURCHASE             43.25
    PAYMENT              30.00
    PURCHASE              7.68
    REFUND               28.97
    PURCHASE             17.86

NEW BALANCE             151.86  DUE
```

Figure 6-16.   A sample billing report for the revolving charge account problem.

Construct a computer program in pseudocode (IPO diagram) that will produce a report for only one customer.

Let us begin by constructing an IPO diagram that describes the solution in broad overview (major subtasks). To do this, we must identify specific subtasks that must be performed. Initially, this may be done without regard to order; they can be placed in order afterward. IPO Diagram 6-4 shows the result of this preliminary analysis in the proper order.

Module M2 in the "Process" portion of IPO Diagram 6-4 may not be obvious. An overpaid balance becomes negative as the balance is calculated, but it is reported as a positive number followed by "CR." Therefore, an overpaid balance must be changed to a negative balance so that it can be used correctly in the calculation of the new balance.

The next step is to construct an IPO diagram for each module. During this step, further subdivision of a module may be necessary, particularly for the loop in M4.

The first module turns out to be a sequence that performs I/O. It is shown in IPO Diagram 6-5.

IPO Diagram 6-4.   Revolving Charge Account Problem

Input	Process	Output
Account number and previous balance with label "CR," "DUE," or blank (with zero balance). Individual transactions with account number, amount, and type (refund, charge, or payment). Trailer record is blank.	M1. Get information from record of last report, and print it. M2. Change overpaid balance to negative. M3. Determine finance charge, and print it. M4. Loop to process transactions. M5. Print new balance with appropriate label. Stop.	Printed report showing account number, previous balance (with label, if required), finance charge, list of transactions (amount and type), and new balance (with label, if required).

IPO Diagram 6-5.   Module 1

Input	Process	Output
Account number and previous balance with label.	Get account number ACCTN, previous balance BAL, and LABEL. Print ACCTN, BAL, and LABEL.	ACCTN, BAL, and LABEL.

In the second module we use selection to determine whether the account is overpaid. This is shown in IPO Diagram 6-6.

IPO Diagram 6-6.   Module 2

Input	Process	Output
BAL and LABEL.	If Label is 'CR', then change BAL to negative BAL. End if.	BAL and LABEL.

We use selection again in the third module: we compute the finance charge only if there is a balance due from the last report.

If the last balance is zero or overpaid, the finance charge is zero. IPO Diagram 6-7 shows this module.

IPO Diagram 6-7.   Module 3

Input	Process	Output
BAL and LABEL.	If LABEL is 'DUE', then finance charge is 2% of BAL. Add finance charge to BAL. Else set finance charge to 0. End if. Print finance charge.	BAL, LABEL, and finance charge.

The fourth module is the loop for processing transactions. First, we must set up the control statements of the loop. The *loop while* construct fits this situation perfectly. Recall that with the *loop while* the item to be tested for terminating the loop must be given a value before the loop is entered, and that it must be given its next value at the bottom of the loop. (See Euclid's algorithm and the largest number problem in Chapter 5.) Since "process transaction" is contained inside the loop module, we will identify it as Module 4-1, meaning that it is a subtask of Module 4. IPO Diagram 6-8 shows the construction of the loop with Module 4-1 shown inside the loop.

IPO Diagram 6-8.   Module 4

Input	Process	Output
Individual transactions with account number, amount, and type.	Get first transaction record: account number, AMOUNT, and TYPE. Loop while record is not blank. M4-1. Process transaction. Get next transaction record: account number, AMOUNT, and TYPE. End loop.	Printed list of transaction records.

The subtask of Module 4 is "process transaction," Module 4-1. What is involved in processing the transaction? The account number obtained with the transaction record must match the original account number (ACCTN). If it does not match, appropriate messages saying so must be printed. If it does match, the amount of the transaction (AMOUNT) must be posted to the balance. Module 4-1 clearly requires a selection unit with two alternative subtasks: Modules 4-1-1 and 4-1-2. (These two modules are subtasks of Module 4-1, which, in turn, is a subtask of Module 4.) IPO Diagram 6-9 shows Module 4-1 with its nested submodules.

IPO Diagram 6-9.   Module 4-1

Input	Process	Output

Account number, AMOUNT, BAL, ACCTN.	If account number does not match ACCTN, then
	    M4-1-1. Print mismatch
	                message.
	
	Else
	    M4-1-2. Post transaction.
	
	End if.
		Printed list of transaction records.

Finally, Modules 4-1-1 and 4-1-2 can be constructed. Module 4-1-1 consists of a sequence of print statements, as shown in IPO Diagram 6-10. Posting the amount of the transaction to the balance (BAL) requires subtracting the amount from BAL in the case of a refund or payment, and adding the amount to BAL in case of a purchase. This requires a selection unit. In both cases the amount and type of the transaction must be printed on the report. Module 4-1-2 is shown in IPO Diagram 6-11.

IPO Diagram 6-10.   Module 4-1-1

Input	Process	Output
Account number, AMOUNT, TYPE.	Print 'account number does not match'. Print account number, AMOUNT, TYPE. Print 'transaction omitted'.	Printed mismatch message.

IPO Diagram 6-11.   Module 4-1-2

Input	Process	Output
TYPE, AMOUNT, BAL.	If TYPE is 'purchase', then add AMOUNT to BAL. Else subtract AMOUNT from BAL. End if. Print AMOUNT and TYPE.	Printed transaction. New BAL.

When Modules 4-1-1 and 4-1-2 have been correctly constructed and tested, we may wish to place them in their proper places in Module 4-1, which then may be placed into Module 4. The completed Module 4 is shown in IPO Diagram 6-12 with boxes around the nested modules to show how they all fit together. (We could just as well have left the modules separate, which would probably be better if Modules 4-1-1 and 4-1-2 had been large.)

The last module (M5) requires printing the new balance of the account. It is possible that the customer has overpaid his or her account (producing a negative balance), that the balance is exactly zero, or that the account has a balance due. It may be necessary to subdivide this subtask, involving nested selection units; but we can probably handle it all together. (It is similar to the double overtime problem in Chapter 5.) IPO Diagram 6-13 shows the result.

We have completed all of the modules. We could combine all of them into one IPO diagram, but it would be long and unwieldy. We would probably have an easier time of it to work from the IPO diagrams of the individual modules, using the "master" process in IPO Diagram 6-4 for their correct sequence. For your convenience, however, the entire process is shown in Figure 6-17. You can see that it does all fit together to make a complete program. You can also see how difficult it would be to try to construct the program in its final form without using a modular approach.

The next step is to translate the complete pseudocode program into a particular programming language. The program must contain at least enough comments to describe clearly the action of each module.

IPO Diagram 6-12.   Module 4, Completed

Input	Process	Output
Individual transactions with account number, AMOUNT, TYPE, and ACCTN.	1. Get first transaction record: account number, AMOUNT, and TYPE. 2. Loop while record is not blank.	Printed list of transaction records (and mismatch message, if required).

M4-1

If account number does not match ACCTN, then

> **M4-1-1**
>
> Print 'account number does not match'.
> Print account number, AMOUNT, TYPE.
> Print 'transaction omitted'.

Else

> **M4-1-2**
>
> if TYPE is 'purchase', then
>   add AMOUNT to BAL.
>
> Else
>
>   subtract AMOUNT from BAL.
>
> End if.
>
> Print AMOUNT and TYPE.

End if.

Get next transaction record: account number, AMOUNT, and TYPE.

End loop.

IPO Diagram 6-13.   Module 5

Input	Process	Output

BAL, LABEL.	If BAL is negative, then change sign of BAL. Set LABEL to 'CR'.
	
	Else
	
	  if BAL is zero, then set LABEL to blank.
	
	  Else
	
	    set LABEL to 'DUE'.
	
	  End if.
	
	End if.
	
	Print BAL and LABEL.
		Printed new balance with correct label.

EXERCISES

1. The temperature conversion problem was used in Chapter 4 to illustrate looping and in Chapter 5 to illustrate selection. Construct a program (IPO diagram) that will read any number of temperatures (one to a record), convert degrees Fahrenheit to degrees centigrade and degrees centigrade to degrees Fahrenheit, and print a table similar to the following table.

Temperature Conversions

25 F	—4 C
0 C	32 F
75 F	24 C
100 F	38 C
—23 C	—9 F
20 C	68 F
100 C	212 F
—40 F	—40 C

Assume that there is a blank trailer record. (Check the units field for blank.)

M1. Get account number ACCTN, previous balance BAL, and
     LABEL. Print ACCTN, BAL, and LABEL.

M2. If LABEL is 'CR', then
          change BAL to negative BAL.
     End if.

M3. If LABEL is 'DUE', then
          finance charge is 2% of BAL.
          Add finance charge to BAL.
     Else
          set finance charge to 0.
     End if.
     Print finance charge.

M4. Get first transaction record: account number, AMOUNT,
     and TYPE.
     Loop while record is not blank.
          If account number does not match ACCTN, then
               Print 'account number does not match'.
               Print account number, AMOUNT, and TYPE.
               Print 'transaction omitted'.
          Else
               if TYPE is 'purchase', then
                    add AMOUNT to BAL.
               Else
                    subtract AMOUNT from BAL.
               End if.
               Print AMOUNT and TYPE.
          End if.
          Get next transaction record: account number,
               AMOUNT, and TYPE.
     End loop.

M5. If BAL is negative, then
          change sign of BAL.
          Set LABEL to 'CR'.
     Else
          if BAL is 0, then
               set LABEL to blank.
          Else
               set LABEL to 'DUE'.
          End if.
     End if.
     Print BAL and LABEL.
     Stop.

Figure 6-17. Complete process for the revolving charge account problem.

Essentially this problem involves placing the program used in Chapter 5 inside the loop used in Chapter 4.

2. Using the IPO diagrams for the revolving charge account problem, place meaningful debugging output statements at the end (or the beginning, if appropriate) of any module where such information would be useful. (Some modules may not need debugging output —Modules 1 and 5, for example. Why?)

3. Expand the revolving charge account problem so that it includes processing for any number of customers. There will be a blank trailer record following each customer's transaction records and an additional blank trailer record following the last customer's trailer record. Construct new IPO diagrams, as required, for the expanded problem. (Do all of the diagrams have to be changed?)

4. Trace the revolving charge account problem with the input records shown in Figure 6-15.

5. Exercise 2 in Chapter 5 presented a simple payroll problem. The program for that problem can be used as a module for a more complex payroll program. Construct a pseudocode program in modular form that will perform the following tasks:

a. Input the Social Security number, name, hours worked, and pay rate.

b. Compute the regular pay, overtime pay (1.5 times the pay rate for all hours over 40), and gross pay.

c. Compute a payroll tax as follows:

$0.00 – $499.99   12%
$500.00 – $749.99   16%
$750.00 – $999.99   20%
$1000.00 and up   24%

d. Print the payroll with appropriate headings, showing the Social Security number, name, hours worked, pay rate, overtime pay, regular pay, gross pay, tax, and net pay for each employee.

e. Program must work for any number of employees. (Use a blank trailer record.)

6. Modify exercise 8 in Chapter 5 so that the program will work for any number of students.

7. Modify exercise 9 in Chapter 5 so that the program will work for any number of customers.

8. Modify the program in exercise 5 (this chapter) by adding one or more modules that accumulate and print at the bottom of the payroll output totals for overtime pay, payroll tax, and gross pay.

9. Perform a trace for the program in exercise 5 using the following data:

111-11-1111	JOE SUDDS	40.0	10.50
222-22-2222	JANE FOAM	52.5	12.95
333-33-3333	JOHN BUGS	35.0	15.00
444-44-4444	JOAN MUGS	60.0	15.00
555-55-5555	JODY JAWS	72.0	12.37

(blank trailer record)

10. Perform a trace for the program in exercise 8 using the data in exercise 9.

11. Construct a flowchart for the process in Figure 6-17. Which seems preferable to you, the flowchart or the pseudocode? Why?

12. You are given a set of records, each containing a student name, course name, and letter grade. There is a record for each course a student has taken, and all of the records have been sorted alphabetically by student name. A few of the records might look like the following:

JOE FRITZ	AMERICAN GOVERNMENT	B
JOE FRITZ	CALCULUS I	A
JOE FRITZ	ENGLISH COMPOSITION I	A
JOE FRITZ	RACQUETBALL	A
JOE FRITZ	COMPUTER PROGRAMMING I	A
JANE GRITZ	INTRO. TO BUSINESS	B
JANE GRITZ	FUND. OF DATA PROCESSING	A
JANE GRITZ	INTERMEDIATE SWIMMING	C
LANE SPITZ	FUND. OF DATA PROCESSING	F
LANE SPITZ	COLLEGE ALGEBRA	D
LANE SPITZ	ENGLISH LITERATURE	D
LANE SPITZ	CHOIR	B

A blank trailer record is used.

Construct a pseudocode program that produces a list with descriptive headings of names, courses, and grades, but having each student name listed only once and a blank line separating students. A sample output for the sample input data is included to show the requirements.

NAME	COURSE	GRADE
JOE FRITZ	AMERICAN GOVERNMENT	B
	CALCULUS I	A
	ENGLISH COMPOSITION I	A
	RACQUETBALL	A
	COMPUTER PROGRAMMING I	A
JANE GRITZ	INTRO. TO BUSINESS	B
	FUND. OF DATA PROCESSING	A
	INTERMEDIATE SWIMMING	C
LANE SPITZ	FUND. OF DATA PROCESSING	F
	COLLEGE ALGEBRA	D
	ENGLISH LITERATURE	D
	CHOIR	B

Apply the techniques used for developing the solution of the savings account problem: identify any selection and repetition modules; identify each subtask and construct a module for it.

13. Suppose that the set of records given in exercise 12 also includes the hours of credit for each course. Compute the grade-point average for each student, letting A, B, C, D, and F be worth 4, 3, 2, 1, and 0, respectively. (The grade-point average is computed by finding the product of credit hours and the value of the letter grade for each course and adding them together, and then dividing the sum by the total number of credit hours.) The following output for one student is a sample of the required output:

NAME	COURSE	GRADE	HOURS
JOE FRITZ	AMERICAN GOVERNMENT	B	3
	CALCULUS I	A	4
	ENGLISH COMPOSITION I	A	3
	RACQUETBALL	A	2

GRADE-POINT AVERAGE 3.75

14. Modify exercise 11 in Chapter 5 so that any number of records may be read. Use the concept of modularity in your program design. Use a blank trailer record.

15. Modify exercise 14 in Chapter 5 so that any number of records may be processed. The required output includes the person's name, the amount of the check, the old balance, and the new balance, as well as the message. Use a blank trailer record.

16. A person borrows $5000 from a bank at 1% interest per month. He makes monthly payments of $200. Construct a computer program in pseudocode that prints the monthly balance and the amount of interest paid each month until the loan is paid off. Remember that the last payment may not be exactly $200. Use modular program design.

17. Construct a computer program in pseudocode that reads a set of records, each containing a test score. Determine the total number of scores and the number of scores in the range

$$80 \leqslant score < 90.$$

Print a message in the following form:

x% OF THE STUDENTS MADE B.

18. Modify exercise 17 in Chapter 5 to work for any number of ads. Use a trailer record of your choice to terminate looping.

19. Construct a computer program in pseudocode that reads a set of records, each containing the name of a tool to be rented, the base rate to rent the tool, and the number of days the tool is rented. Print the name of the tool, the days rented, and the cost to rent it. Calculate the cost using the following table:

Day 1	100% of base rate
Days 2–5	65% of base rate per day
Days 6–15	150% of base rate per day

Use a trailer record of your choice.

20. Modify exercise 19 in Chapter 5 so that any number of records can be processed. Use a trailer record of your choice, and use modular program design.

21. Using the tax rules in exercise 20 of Chapter 5, construct a computer program in pseudocode that gets an employee's name, Social Security number (SSN), and annual salary and prints the name, SSN, annual salary, and income tax for a set of records with a blank trailer record. Printed output must be in tabular form with column headings, and the totals of the annual salaries and the income taxes must be printed at the bottom of the table in their respective columns.

7 LOOP WITH COUNTER

We can count, but we are rapidly forgetting
how to say what is worth counting and why.

Joseph Weizenbaum
Computer Power and Human Reason

I own the stars, because nobody else
before me ever thought of owning them.

Antoine de Saint-Exupéry
The Little Prince

A loop that is to be repeated a certain number of times is useful in many cases. This type of loop requires a counter, which is tested against some limit that is the number of times the loop is to be performed. A special case of the repetition unit provides automatic counting and testing. This type of repetition unit is called by different names: *indexed repetition, indexed loop, loop with index,* or *loop with counter.* We shall use *loop with counter* since it is the most descriptive.

In Chapter 4 we introduced a version of the temperature conversion program that produced a table starting at 0° F and ending with 100° F, in one-degree intervals (see IPO Diagram 7-1). This program actually contains a degree counter that counts from 0 to 100, inclusive.

IPO Diagram 7-1.   Temperature Conversion Table in One-Degree Increments

Input	Process	Output
None.	1. Print column headings: 'Degrees F' and 'Degrees C'. 2. Set F to 0. 3. Loop while F is less than or equal to 100. Compute C. Print F and C. Add 1 to F. End loop. 4. Stop	Table of temperatures, showing degrees F and degrees C in one-degree increments, from 0° F to 100° F.

In Chapter 6 we presented the savings account problem, which contains a year counter, counting from one to the number of years, inclusive (see IPO Diagram 7-2).

In each of these examples the value of the counter is used to terminate looping. These loops are being performed a certain number of times; they are loops with counters. We can easily use the *loop with counter* construct in these examples. But first let us examine the construct.

STRUCTURE OF THE *LOOP WITH COUNTER*

The counter is the principal feature of the *loop with counter.* We give the counter a name, just as we would name any other value. The counter must be given its *initial value* (or *initialized*) before looping begins. As each pass through the loop is made, the counter must be updated—that is, it must count. We usually refer to this as *incrementing* the counter. Each time the counter is updated, it must also be *tested* against the limit (or test value) for loop termination. Three important words summarize what must be done to the counter: *initialize, increment,* and *test.*

We may initialize the counter to any appropriate value for a particular application, but we usually start at one. The actual incrementing is done by the computer in the *loop with counter* construct,

IPO Diagram 7-2.   Savings Account Problem

Input	Process	Output
Amount deposited.	Get deposit, interest rate, and number of years.	Deposit.
Rate of interest.		Interest rate.
Number of years.	Print with descriptive labels deposit, interest rate, and number of years.	Number of years.
		For each year:
	Print column headings.	year
	Move deposit to old balance.	old balance
		interest
		new balance.
	Divide interest rate by 100.	
		All with descriptive labels and headings.
	Set year to 1.	
	Loop while year is less than or equal to number of years.	
	Compute interest by multiplying interest rate by old balance.	
	Compute new balance by adding interest to old balance.	
	Print a line of the table (year, old balance, interest, new balance).	
	Add 1 to year.	
	Move new balance to old balance.	
	End loop.	
	Stop.	

but we must set the size of the increment. The size of the increment may be any appropriate number, but it is usually one. The computer also does the testing in the *loop with counter*, but we must set the limit. The limit may also be any number, but it is usually the number of times that the loop is to be performed (assuming that the counter is initialized to one and incremented by one).

The counter must be initialized before the body of the loop is entered. The increment and test may be at the top of the loop or at the bottom, depending on the particular programming language being used. In either case, looping is terminated when the value of the counter exceeds the test value. (The only important problem arising from the position of the increment and test actions is what happens when the initial value of the counter exceeds the test value. In this case, if incrementing and testing are at the bottom of the loop, the body of the loop is performed once, as in the *loop until*. On the other hand, if the incrementing and testing are at the top of the loop, the body of the loop is not performed at all, as in the *loop while*.) We shall assume that the test is at the top.

Some computer languages allow *decrementing*, which is counting backwards, or "incrementing" with negative numbers. In this case looping is terminated when the value of the counter is less than the test value. We shall concern ourselves only with incrementing (positive).

PSEUDOCODE FOR *LOOP WITH COUNTER*

In pseudocode the *loop with counter* is specified by the key words *loop for*, followed by the name of the counter and its initial value, test value, and increment value. The bottom of the loop is delineated by *end loop*, as in all other cases of repetition units.

The *loop for* statement must include the name of the counter and its initial, test, and increment values. The general form of the *loop for* statement may be stated as follows:

Loop for *name* = *i* **to** *j* **by** *k*

where *name* is replaced by the name of the counter, *i* is replaced by the initial value (or its name, if a variable value is used), *j* is replaced by the test value (or its name), and *k* is replaced by the increment value (or its name). If the value of the increment is one, then *by k* may be omitted. A missing increment is always understood to mean that the increment value is one.

Figure 7-1 shows the general form of the *loop with counter*. Whenever the value of the counter becomes larger than *j*, the test condition for termination is met. At that time the statement immediately following *end loop* is executed, as with all other repetition units.

```
Loop for name = i to j by k.

    Body of loop

End loop.
```

Figure 7-1. General form of the loop *with counter. Name is replaced by the name of the counter;* i, j, *and* k *are replaced by the initial, test, and increment values (or their names), respectively.*

THE TEMPERATURE CONVERSION TABLE

Now we can restructure the process in IPO Diagram 7-1 using a *loop with counter*. Figure 7-2 shows only those statements in the process that control looping—that is, the ones that initialize, increment, and test the counter named F. These three statements can be replaced by a single *loop for* statement. Notice that specifying the increment is optional since it is one.

```
Initialize: Set F to 0.

Test:       Loop while F is less than or equal to 100.

                . . .

Increment:      Add 1 to F.

            End loop.

Loop for F = 0 to 100 by 1.              Loop for F = 0 to 100

        . . .                or              . . .

End loop,                                 End loop.
```

Figure 7-2. Statements from IPO Diagram 7-1 that control looping, with their equivalent loop *with counter construct.*

IPO Diagram 7-3 shows the revised program.

IPO Diagram 7-3.   Temperature Conversion Table in One-Degree Increments

Input	Process	Output
None.	1. Print column headings: 'Degrees F' and 'Degrees C'. 2. Loop for F = 0 to 100 by 1. Compute C. Print F and C. End loop. 3. Stop.	Table of temperatures, showing degrees F and degrees C, in one-degree increments from 0° F to 100° F.

THE SAVINGS ACCOUNT PROBLEM

The program for the savings account problem can be treated in a similar manner. Figure 7-3 shows the statements that control looping and their respective *loop for* statement. IPO Diagram 7-4 shows the revised program.

Initialize: Set year to 1.

Test: Loop while year is less than or equal to number of years.

. . .

Increment: Add 1 to year.

. . .

          End loop.

Loop for year = 1 to number of years.

. . .

End loop.

Figure 7-3. Statements from IPO Diagram 7-2 that control looping, with their equivalent loop with counter *construct.*

IPO Diagram 7-4.   Savings Account Problem

Input	Process	Output
Amount deposited. Rate of interest. Number of years.	Get deposit, interest rate, and number of years. Print with descriptive labels deposit, interest rate, and number of years. Print column headings. Move deposit to old balance. Divide interest rate by 100. Loop for year = 1 to number of years. 　　Compute interest by multiplying interest rate by old balance. 　　Compute new balance by adding interest to old balance. 　　Print a line of the table (year, old balance, interest, new balance). 　　Move new balance to old balance. End loop. Stop.	Deposit. Interest rate. Number of years. For each year: 　year 　old balance 　interest 　new balance. All with descriptive labels and headings.

PRODUCING A TABLE OF SQUARES AND SQUARE ROOTS

Before the advent of electronic computers, producing large tables of numbers (such as trigonometric tables, logarithm tables, navigation tables, and ballistic tables) was a dreadfully time-consuming task. It was not uncommon for people to spend years constructing tables by hand. One of the first electronic computers, the ENIAC (1946), was developed as a result of the U.S. Army's need for ballistic tables during World War II. (Although ENIAC was too late to help the war effort, it was the forerunner in the new era of information processing.)

Tables can be produced with a modern computer more quickly than they can be printed. Even the beginning programmer can instruct a computer to produce numerical tables. We shall now construct a program to produce a table that contains the squares and square roots of the numbers 1–1000. It turns out to be a simple task. Just as inexpensive hand-held calculators usually have a square root function, computers also have "built-in" programs that do a number of common tasks, including extracting square roots. We can simply use the square root function. (This is done differently in different computer languages, but that is not our concern here. "Compute square root" is sufficient in pseudocode.)

Since we need the numbers 1–1000, we can make good use of the *loop with counter*. We must have a counter that has an initial value of 1, a test value of 1000, and an increment of 1.

A program to produce the required table is shown in IPO Diagram 7-5. Notice that in the *loop for* statement, the increment is omitted, indicating that it is 1. The statement could have also been written

Loop for N = 1 to 1000 by 1.

IPO Diagram 7-5.   Table of Squares and Square Roots for Numbers 1-1000

Input	Process	Output

None.	1. Print table headings.
	
	2. Loop for N = 1 to 1000.
	    Compute the square of N (N^2).
	    Compute the square root of N.
	    Print N, square of N, and
	    square root of N.
	    End loop.
	
	3. Stop.
		Printed table of squares and square roots of numbers 1-1000.

This program is not a generally useful one. We need to construct a program that can be used for any numbers with any increment value. We can easily construct such a program. Suppose, for example, that we need a table of squares and square roots of only the even numbers in the interval 10–100. We can generalize the program so that starting, stopping, and increment values can be input from a card or a keyboard. Whenever possible, input values must be checked to make sure that they are reasonable, so that errors made while entering data can be detected. We can do this by requiring the starting value to be less than the stopping value. We should also require the starting value to be positive (no square roots of negative numbers) and the increment value to be greater than zero.

The program now consists of a selection unit with an alternative module that prints messages concerning erroneous input information and an alternative module that produces the table.

Since there are three requirements for the input data, we will use a selection containing a *compound* test: if the initial value is less than or equal to the stopping value *or* the initial value is less than zero *or* the increment value is less than or equal to zero, then. . . . If at least one of these conditions is met, something is wrong with the input data, and the table cannot be produced. IPO Diagram 7-6 summarizes the program.

IPO Diagram 7-6. General Table of Squares and Square Roots

Input	*Process*	*Output*

Initial value, test value, and increment value.	1. Get initial value INIT, test value LAST, and increment value INC.
	
	 2. If INIT $\geqslant$ LAST or INIT $<$ 0 or INC $\leqslant$ 0, then
	   2.1 Print error messages.
	Else
	   2.2 Print table.
	End if.
	
	 3. Stop.
		Printed table of squares and square roots of numbers.

Module 2-1 is simple enough to construct. Module 2-2 has already been constructed in the IPO diagram for producing the table for numbers 1–1000. Only modifications to the *loop for* statement have to be made. IPO Diagram 7-7 shows the completed program.

IPO Diagram 7-7.   Complete Program for Table of Squares and Square Roots

Input	Process	Output

Initial value, test value, and increment value.	1. Get initial value INIT, test value LAST, and increment value INC.
	
	2. If INIT $\geq$ LAST or INIT $<$ 0 or INC $\leq$ 0, then
	    print "Error in input data."
	    Print INIT, LAST, and INC with labels.
	Else
	    print table headings.
	    Loop for N = INIT to LAST by INC.
	        Compute square of N.
	        Compute square root of N.
	        Print N, square of N, and square root of N.
	    End loop.
	End if.
	
	3. Stop.
		Printed table of squares and square roots of numbers.

USE OF A HEADER RECORD

We have frequently used a trailer record (such as a blank record) as a signal to terminate looping. Now that we have the *loop with counter*, we can examine a second way of controlling looping with input information: the *header record*. We can place a header record in front of the input records; it indicates the number of records (or items of data) that follow it. Let us consider, for example, the largest number problem from Chapter 5. In that problem we were given a stack of records (cards), each containing a number; a blank trailer record was used to indicate when to stop reading. The IPO diagram for that program is reproduced in IPO Diagram 7-8.

Instead of using a trailer record, let us now place a header record in front of the records; on that record we shall place the number of records that follow. For example, the header record would contain ten if there were ten records containing values of N. The value on the header record, then, could be used as the test value in a *loop for* statement. IPO Diagram 7-9 shows how the program could be constructed using a header record.

IPO Diagram 7-8.   The Largest Number (Blank Trailer Record)

Input	Process	Output

Records (cards) with number on each.	1. Read N from first record.
	
	2. Print N.
	
	3. Save N in MAX.
	
	4. Read N from next record.
	
	5. Loop while record is not blank.
	    Print N.
	    If N is larger than MAX, then
	      save N in MAX.
	    End if.
	    Read N from next record.
	    End loop.
	
	6. Write 'Largest number is ', MAX.
	
	7. Stop.
		Largest number.

IPO Diagram 7-9.   The Largest Number (Header Record)

Input	Process	Output

Header record with number of records following it.
 	
Records with number on each.
	1. Get number of records (NRECORDS) from header record.
	
	2. Read N from next record.
	
	3. Print N.
	
	4. Save N in MAX.
	
	5. Loop for J = 2 to NRECORDS.
	    Read N from next record.
	    Print N.
	    If N is larger than MAX, then
	      save N in MAX.
	    End if.
	    End loop.
	
	6. Print 'Largest number is ', MAX.
	
	7. Stop.
		Largest number.

Why is the counter J initialized to 2 in the *loop for* statement? The first value of N is read in step 2; therefore, the loop counter must begin at 2.

THE AVERAGE OF SOME NUMBERS

The *loop with counter* can also be used to compute the sum of some numbers. Consider the same input as the largest number problem, but this time we want to find the average value of the numbers. To do this, we must compute the sum of the numbers and divide it by the number of numbers. The value of the sum (a *cumulative* or *running* sum) must be initialized (in this case, to zero) before the loop is entered. A program to find the average of the numbers is shown in IPO Diagram 7-10.

IPO Diagram 7-10.   Average of Some Numbers

Input	Process	Output
Header record with number of records following it. Records with number on each.	1. Set sum to 0. 2. Get number of records (NRECORDS) from header record. Loop for J = 1 to NRECORDS. Read N from next record. Print N. Add N to sum. End loop. 3. Average is sum/NRECORDS. 4. Print average, with label. 5. Stop.	Average value of the input numbers.

TRANSLATING THE *LOOP WITH COUNTER* INTO A COMPUTER LANGUAGE

Most commonly used programming languages provide a means of implementing a loop with a counter. Translating pseudocode into one of these languages should be straightforward. (The *loop with counter* can, of course, be implemented using the general loop of Chapter 4. With the general loop, it is up to the programmer to initialize, increment, and test the counter explicitly.) Some languages increment and test at the top of the loop; others increment and test at the bottom. Some allow only positive increment values, whereas others allow negative increment values as well. Various constraints may also be placed on the initial and test values; for example, they may be allowed to be only nonzero and positive. Consult the textbook or manual for the language you are using for details.

You will need to determine how to use the built-in square root function, which you can probably find in the index of your textbook or manual. Find out what other built-in functions are available.

EXERCISES

In the following exercises initialize the sum before the loop is entered.

1. Construct a computer program in pseudocode (IPO diagram) that will compute the sum of the numbers 1–100 and print the result.

2. Repeat exercise 1 for the numbers 101–1000.

3. Construct a computer program in pseudocode (IPO diagram) that will print a list of the even numbers 8–100 and compute and print their sum.

4. Construct a computer program in pseudocode (IPO diagram) that will compute the sum of the first 20 terms of the expression

$$1 + \frac{1}{2} + \frac{1}{3} + \frac{1}{4} + \ldots$$

(The sum may be given an initial value of 1 or 0. Why? Another point to notice is that the first term (1) can also be thought of as 1/1 so that it looks like the rest of the terms. Which initial value of the sum is better?)

5. The Fibonacci sequence was described in exercise 8 of Chapter 4. We can use a *loop with counter* to generate a Fibonacci sequence

containing a certain number of elements. Construct a computer program in pseudocode that will print the first 30 numbers of the Fibonacci sequence.

6. Modify the program in exercise 5 so that it prints only the 30th through the 50th elements of the Fibonacci sequence.

7. In exercise 1 of Chapter 6 we used a trailer record to terminate looping. Reconstruct the program so that a header record giving the number of items to be processed is used.

8. Construct a computer program in pseudocode that prints a multiplication table for any number n and the numbers 1 through m, where n and m are input values. The table should appear as follows if n is 3 and m is 4:

$3 \times 1 = 3$

$3 \times 2 = 6$

$3 \times 3 = 9$

$3 \times 4 = 12$

9. A single-celled organism divides to become two single-celled creatures every four hours. Those two divide into four, which divide into eight, and so on. Construct a computer program in pseudocode that prints the time starting at 12:00 A.M. (actually 0:00), the day starting with 1 January, and the number of organisms starting at 1. Print the day, time, and number of organisms after each division—every four hours—for the month of January.

10. Perform a trace for the program in IPO Diagram 7-4 with a deposit of $200 at 7.5% interest for five years.

11. Suppose the Bank of Utopia pays 100% interest compounded daily. If you deposit a penny, in how many days will you become a millionaire? Construct a computer program in pseudocode that will determine the answer.

12. Modify the program in IPO Diagram 7-3 so that the table can begin and end with any temperature and any increment can be used.

13. There is no standard flowchart symbol for the *loop with counter*. However, a convenient symbol is shown in the following flowchart, in which C is the counter and i, j, and k are the initial, test, and increment values, respectively.

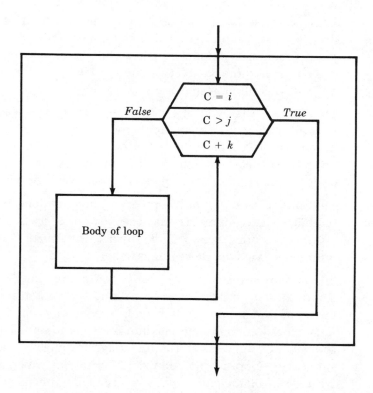

Construct a flowchart for the process in IPO Diagram 7-3.

14. In exercise 11 of Chapter 4 an inventory list was printed. A blank trailer record was used. Modify this problem so that a header record containing the number of items in the inventory is used instead of the trailer record. Use a *loop with counter* to control looping.

15. In exercise 12 of Chapter 4 a list of names and addresses was printed, and a line number was printed with each line. Modify the problem so that, instead of using a blank trailer record, we use a header record containing the number of names in the list. Use a *loop with counter* to control looping and also to generate the line numbers.

16. In exercise 10 of Chapter 4 the balance of a savings account was printed. Modify the problem so that it prints the balance for 100 days. Use a *loop with counter* to control looping and to generate the day.

17. In exercise 18 of Chapter 4 some rules for the fine for an overdue library book were given. Using these same rules, construct a computer program in pseudocode that prints a table showing the day, the daily fine, and the cumulative fine for 100 days. The table must have a title and column headings.

18. Suppose that you are given a set of records, each containing a person's name and phone number (a "phone book"), and you would like a sample of the population on which to conduct a telephone poll. Construct a computer program in pseudocode that reads the phone book and prints every seventh name and phone number.

19. Construct a computer program in pseudocode that prints a sequence of 15 numbers that are powers of two—that is, the first number is 1, the second 2, the third 4, the fourth 8, and so on. Each number is twice the preceding number.

20. You are given a set of records containing daily weather data for a month. The header record contains the first three letters of the name of the month and the number of days in the month. Each data record contains the maximum and minimum temperatures and the amount of rainfall for one day. Produce a monthly weather summary report in the following format, in which x's are replaced by relevant data and *mon* is replaced by the name of the month abbreviated to the first three letters:

WEATHER SUMMARY FOR mon

DAY	MAXI-MUM TEMP.	MINI-MUM TEMP.	RAINFALL	CUMULATIVE RAINFALL
xx	xxx	xxx	xx.xx	xx.xx
xx	xxx	xxx	xx.xx	xx.xx
AVERAGES	xxx	xxx	xx.xx	

Below the table print the average maximum and minimum temperatures and the average rainfall in their respective columns.

21. Construct a computer program in pseudocode that prints a table containing the radius, circumference, and area for each circle with radius 1, 2, 3, . . . , 25. The circumference of a circle is found by multiplying 2 times π (3.14159) times radius. The area of a circle is found by multiplying π times the square of the radius. Place descriptive headings in the table.

ARRAYS OF ONE DIMENSION

8

We often have to deal with various pieces of information that have one or more distinguishing characteristics in common. For example, suppose that we would like to know the average age of the people living in a community of 100 people. There would be 100 pieces of information—that is, 100 ages. The common property of each piece of information is that it represents an age. We could describe each piece of information simply as an *age*. Yet each number is distinct from all other ages; each age is that of a specific person, and is generally different in value from the other ages. Thus, each age has two properties: one is shared in common with all of the others (it is an *age*), and the other is unique (it refers to the age of a *specific* person).

DEFINITION OF AN ARRAY

A grouping of items that have a similar characteristic or an identifying property in common is called an *array*. Each item in the array
is referred to as an *element* of the array. Each element is uniquely
identified by a number called a *subscript*, designating its position
in the array. An array whose elements have only one subscript is
said to be *one-dimensional*. (It can be thought of as having only the
one dimension of length.) Within the context of computers, since
computers process information, an array is a group of items of
information that have some characteristic in common.

Examples of arrays are numerous, but we can consider a few of
them: seats in an auditorium, people in a room, freshmen in a
residence hall, apples in a market, books on a shelf, peas in a pod,
and the 12 days of Christmas. The calendar is an interesting example
of arrays: days in a month, days in a year, days in a week, months in
a year, weeks in a year, years in a century, and so on.

In each of the examples cited, each item shares one or more
properties in common with the other items in the same array; yet
each is distinct from the others by its position in the array. For
example, the seats in an auditorium are all seats, but each is in a
different position in the auditorium. In the same way, a day of a
month is distinct from the other days in the month by its position
in the month. *The notion that the position of an element in an array
distinguishes it from a host of similar elements is essential for understanding and using arrays.*

In order to clarify the terms *array*, *element*, and *subscript*, let
us consider some examples of arrays and what can be done with
them.

AN EXAMPLE OF AN ARRAY OF EGGS

The eggs in an egg carton constitute an array. Each egg has its "egg-
ness" in common with the other eggs. Yet each egg is distinct from
the others in its size, weight, color, texture, or shape, or any combination of these—and by its position among the other eggs. In an egg
carton we can refer to each egg uniquely by a subscript, as illustrated

in Figure 8-1. Each egg is different from the others in that it occupies a unique position. Thus, we can specify "egg 1" with no ambiguity. "Egg 1" is certainly not "egg 8," even though they may look alike.

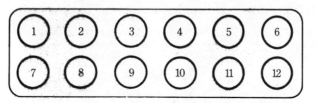

Figure 8-1. A carton of eggs, illustrating an array of eggs. The numbers indicate positions in the array, numbered sequentially.

In the terminology of arrays, we would specify a particular egg as "egg-sub-one" or "egg-sub-ten," written egg_1 and egg_{10} in mathematical notation, or as $egg(1)$ and $egg(10)$ in pseudocode notation.

Suppose we wish to find the average weight of the eggs in a carton. We can let W followed by a subscript represent the weight of each egg. We would then have an array of weights whose name is W. Suppose the eggs have the following weights in grams:

W(1) W(2) W(3) W(4) W(5) W(6) W(7) W(8) W(9) W(10) W(11) W(12)

  63   60   62   58   56   61   62   59   57   60   63   61

Then the array W consists of the following numbers:

   63   60   62   58   56   61   62   59   57   60   63   61

We can find the average weight by computing

$$\frac{W(1)+W(2)+W(3)+W(4)+W(5)+W(6)+W(7)+W(8)+W(9)+W(10)+W(11)+W(12)}{12}$$

or

$$\frac{63 + 60 + 62 + 58 + 56 + 61 + 62 + 59 + 57 + 60 + 63 + 61}{12} = \frac{722}{12}$$

The process of adding the weights is tedious when done this way. It is a repetitious task, which suggests the possibility of a repetition module performed by a computer. In fact, the problem can be solved easily with the aid of a computer and the *loop with counter*. IPO Diagram 8-1 shows how it can be done.

IPO Diagram 8-1.   The Average of an Array of Numbers

Input	Process	Output
12 weights.	1. Declare W to be an array of 12 elements.	Average weight.
	2. Loop for J = 1 to 12. Get W(J). Print 'W(',J,') is ', W(J). End loop.	
	3. Set SUM to 0.	
	4. Loop for J = 1 to 12. Add W(J) to SUM. End loop.	
	5. Compute average: SUM/12.	
	6. Print average, with label.	
	7. Stop.	

Notice in step 2 that when J is 1, W(1) is read; when J is 2, W(2) is read; and so forth, until W(12) has been read. In step 4, when J is 1, W(1) is added to SUM; when J is 2, W(2) is added to SUM; and so forth, until W(12) has been added to SUM. Computing the average this way is quite painless.

In step 1 of the process, W was declared to be an array. This step is important and, in general, must be performed in some manner in the various computer languages. When arrays are used in pseudo-code, such a declaration must be made so that it will not be forgotten when translating pseudocode into a computer language.

THE LARGEST NUMBER PROBLEM

In Chapter 7 the *loop with counter* was used in the program for finding the largest number of a set of numbers. The set of numbers can be thought of in terms of an array. We can place all of the numbers into an array and then find the largest number (element) in the array. IPO Diagram 8-2 shows one way to do this.

IPO Diagram 8-2.   The Largest Element of an Array of Numbers

Input	Process	Output

Header record with number of elements in an array of numbers.
 	
 An array of numbers.
	1. Declare N to be an array.
	
	 2. Get number of elements NUM from header record.
	
	 3. Loop for J = 1 to NUM.
	    Get N(J).
	    Print 'N(',J,') = ', N(J).
	End loop.
	
	 4. Save N(1) in MAX.
	
	 5. Loop for J = 2 to NUM.
	    If N(J) is larger than MAX,
	    then
	        save N(J) in MAX.
	    End if.
	End loop.
	
	 6. Print 'Largest number is ', MAX.
	
	 7. Stop.
		Largest number.

In most cases when an array is used, all of the elements of the array are input together in a single module. After the input is completed, the elements of the array are processed in whatever way is necessary for accomplishing the required task.

A SIMPLE SORTING ALGORITHM

Sorting an array into ascending (alphabetical, when dealing with alphabetic elements such as names) or descending order is a common application of computers. Sorting algorithms can be complicated, and much research has gone and continues to go into their development. There are, however, some simple (but inefficient) sorting algorithms. One of these is the *bubble sort*.

The bubble sort consists of passing through an array, comparing each successive pair of elements, interchanging pairs that are out of order, and repeating this process until the array is in order. The time required to sort an array of N elements this way is proportional to N^2, making the bubble sort inefficient for arrays with many elements. The time requirement is tolerable, however, when dealing with arrays of few elements—that is, for small values of N. The initial order of an array also may affect the time required to sort it.

A nice feature that can be incorporated into the bubble sort is the ability to quit when the array is sorted. This can be done by using a *program switch*. A switch is simply a named value that is tested in order to determine which action to take in a program. For example, the switch may be allowed to have values of zero and one. When it is zero, one action is taken; when it is one, another action is taken. The flow of control through a program can be altered by changing the value of the switch.

IPO Diagram 8-3 shows a program to sort an array of elements into ascending (increasing) order.

IPO Diagram 8-3.   Bubble Sort (Ascending Order)

Input	Process	Output

Header record with number of elements in an array.
 	
An array of numbers.
	1. Declare AR to be an array.
	
	2. Get NUM, the number of elements in the array.
	
	3. Print 'Array before sorting'.
	
	4. Loop for J = 1 to NUM.
	     Get AR(J).
	     Print AR(J).
	     End loop.
	
	5. Set switch to 1.
	
	6. Loop while switch is 1.
	     Set switch to 0.
	     Loop for J = 1 to (NUM − 1).
	      If AR(J) > AR(J + 1), then
	       interchange AR(J)
	       and AR(J + 1).
	       Set switch to 1.
	      End if.
	     End loop.
	     End loop.
	
	7. Print 'Sorted array'.
	
	8. Loop for J = 1 to NUM.
	     Print AR(J).
	     End loop.
	
	9. Stop.
		An array arranged in ascending order.

Figure 8-2 illustrates a trace through the process for an array of five elements: 5, 10, 3, 8, and 6. Successive pairs of elements are compared; they are interchanged if they are out of order. Any time an interchange is performed, the switch is set to 1, to indicate that something was out of order. At the end of each pass, the switch is tested. If it is 1, meaning that something was out of order, it is reset to 0 and another pass is begun. If it is 0, the array is in order and sorting is terminated.

First pass.   *Switch 0.*

5 } In	5	5	5	5
10 } order	10 } Inter-	3	3	3
3	3 } change	10 } Inter-	8	8
8	8	8 } change	10 } Inter-	6
6	6	6	6 } change	10

Switch 1 (repeat)

Second pass.   *Switch 0.*

5 } Inter-	3	3	3
3 } change	5 } In	5	5
8	8 } order	8 } Inter-	6
6	6	6 } change	8 } In
10	10	10	10 } order

Switch 1 (repeat)

Third pass.   *Switch 0.*

3 } In	3	3	3
5 } order	5 } In	5	5
6	6 } order	6 } In	6
8	8	8 } order	8 } In
10	10	10	10 } order

Switch 0 (quit)

Figure 8-2.   Trace of a bubble sort (IPO Diagram 8-3), showing the comparisons and interchanges during each pass, and the value of the program switch before and after each pass.

Figure 8-3 summarizes the results at the end of each pass. It is important that you follow the trace through carefully until you see exactly what is happening.

						Switch	
Original array	5	10	3	8	6	1	(repeat)
End of first pass	5	3	8	6	10	1	(repeat)
End of second pass	3	5	6	8	10	1	(repeat)
End of third pass	3	5	6	8	10	0	(quit)

Figure 8-3.   Bubble sort. Results at the end of each pass.

We can improve the program. At the end of the first pass the largest element is in the last position of the array. (Confirm this in Figure 8-2). Since it is now in its correct position, there is no longer any need to compare it to the preceding element. For the second pass we can omit the last element. Similarly, at the end of the second pass, the next-to-largest element is in the next-to-last position; we can omit it, along with the last element, for the third pass. We can continue in this manner until there are only two elements remaining, the first and second. To do this, we define another value named LIMIT that will limit the number of times the body of the inner loop (*loop with counter*) is performed. IPO Diagram 8-4 includes this modification.

In this case there are two criteria for terminating looping in the outer loop. When the value of either LIMIT or the switch is zero, looping is terminated.

Figure 8-4 shows a trace of the program with the refinement of omitting large elements as they collect at the bottom. In this example looping is terminated because the value of the switch is zero. The value of LIMIT becomes zero and terminates looping in the case of an array whose elements are initially arranged in reverse order.

IPO Diagram 8-4.   Bubble Sort with Refinement (Ascending Order)

Input	Process	Output
Header record with number of elements in an array. An array of numbers.	1. Declare AR to be an array. 2. Get NUM, the number of elements in the array. 3. Print 'Array before sorting'. 4. Loop for J = 1 to NUM. Get AR(J). Print AR(J). End loop. 5. Set LIMIT to (NUM − 1). 6. Set switch to 1. 7. Loop while switch is 1 and LIMIT > 0. Set switch to 0. Loop for J = 1 to LIMIT. If AR(J) > AR(J + 1), then interchange AR(J) and AR(J + 1). Set switch to 1. End if. End loop. Subtract 1 from LIMIT. End loop. 8. Print 'Sorted array'. 9. Loop for J = 1 to NUM. Print AR(J). End loop. 10. Stop.	An array arranged in ascending order.

Pass 1.   Switch 0.   LIMIT 4.

5	In order	5		5		5		5
10		10	Inter-change	3		3		3
3		3		10	Inter-change	8		8
8		8		8		10	Inter-change	6
6		6		6		6		10

Switch 1 (repeat)

Pass 2.   Switch 0.   LIMIT 3.

5	Inter-change	3		3		3
3		5	In order	5		5
8		8		8	Inter-change	6
6		6		6		8
—		—		—		—
10	Omit	10		10		10

Switch 1 (repeat)

Pass 3.   Switch 0.   LIMIT 2.

3	In order	3	
5		5	In order
6		6	
—		—	
8	Omit	8	
10		10	

Switch 0 (quit)

Figure 8-4. Trace of a bubble sort with the refinement of omitting large elements as they collect at the bottom (IPO Diagram 8-4).

An important question to raise is, "What happens if there is only one element in the array?" (It is already "sorted.") If NUM is one, LIMIT is set to zero. Since LIMIT is not greater than zero, the loop is bypassed, and the single element is printed.

INTERCHANGING TWO VALUES

We have been using the term *interchange*. How are two elements interchanged? Figure 8-5 illustrates one way to interchange the values stored in AR(J) and AR(J + 1). A temporary storage location (TEMP) must be used to hold one of the elements during the interchange. The interchange process for a general case is shown in IPO Diagram 8-5.

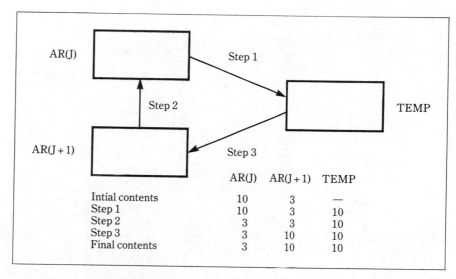

	AR(J)	AR(J + 1)	TEMP
Intial contents	10	3	—
Step 1	10	3	10
Step 2	3	3	10
Step 3	3	10	10
Final contents	3	10	10

Figure 8-5.   Interchanging two elements of an array.

IPO Diagram 8-5.   Interchanging Values in Two Storage Locations (Interchanging the Contents of Two Storage Locations)

Input	Process	Output
Two numbers, J and K.	1. Save J in TEMP. 2. Save K in J. 3. Save TEMP in K.	Values of J and K interchanged.

THE SUM OF TWO ARRAYS

The sum of two arrays is defined to be the array containing the sum of the corresponding elements of the arrays. (The two arrays must have the same number of elements and the same dimension.) IPO Diagram 8-6 shows a program that computes the sum of two arrays named A and B and stores the sum in an array named C.

IPO Diagram 8-6.   The Sum of Two Arrays

Input	Process	Output
Header record with number of elements in arrays A and B. An array A. An array B.	1. Declare A, B, and C to be arrays. 2. Get number of elements N. 3. Loop for J = 1 to N. Get A(J). End loop. 4. Loop for J = 1 to N. Get B(J). End loop. 5. Loop for J = 1 to N. C(J) = A(J) + B(J). End loop. 6. Print column headings: 'Array A', 'Array B', 'Sum'. 7. Loop for J = 1 to N. Print A(J), B(J), C(J). End loop. 8. Stop.	The sum of two arrays.

TRANSLATING PSEUDOCODE FOR ARRAYS INTO A COMPUTER LANGUAGE

Programming languages differ in their notation for arrays, but the notation we have been using in pseudocode is used in many of them. Some languages have restrictions on subscripts; others do not. Some kind of statement is required for declaring a name to be the name of an array and to indicate the maximum number of elements to be expected. You can find out what is required for the programming language you are using by looking up *arrays* (one-dimensional) in the index or table of contents of your textbook or manual.

EXERCISES

1. Perform a trace on the process in IPO Diagram 8-4 for the case of an array containing two elements (NUM is 2). What causes looping to be terminated?

2. Perform a trace on the process in IPO Diagram 8-4 for the following array:

| 10 | 15 | 4 | 25 | 70 | 34 | 5 | 11 | 43 | 26 |

What causes looping to be terminated?

3. Perform a trace on the process in IPO Diagram 8-4 for the following array:

| 23 | 20 | 18 | 16 | 11 | 10 |

What causes looping to be terminated?

4. Perform a trace on the process in IPO Diagram 8-4 for the following array:

| 10 | 11 | 16 | 18 | 20 | 23 |

What causes looping to be terminated?

5. Construct a program (IPO diagram) that will arrange an array of numbers in descending order.

6. How should array elements that are equal be handled during sorting? Perform a trace on the process in IPO Diagram 8-4 for the following array:

| 10 | 15 | 5 | 10 | 25 | 5 |

7. Euclid's algorithm for finding the greatest common divisor was discussed in Chapter 4. In that case the two input numbers were assumed to be in ascending order—the smaller followed by the larger. Let us remove that restriction and allow them to be in either order. Add to the program a module that will place them in the correct order if necessary. What happens if the two numbers are equal?

8. The Fibonacci sequence was defined in exercise 8 of Chapter 4. Construct a computer program in pseudocode that generates an array containing 30 elements of the Fibonacci sequence, finds their sum, and prints the sequence and the sum.

9. Given three numbers, construct a computer program in pseudocode that arranges the numbers in descending order. Do not use the bubble sort.

10. Construct a computer program in pseudocode that grades multiple-choice tests. The number of questions (maximum 50) is on the first record, and the correct responses are on the second record. A set of records follows, each containing a student's name and test responses. A blank trailer record is used. Place the correct responses into an array, and place each student's responses into another array. Compare responses and count the number correct. Print a list of names and test scores.

11. Suppose that a text consisting of 50 characters is read from a record. Construct a computer program in pseudocode that counts the number of times the letter E occurs in the text. The characters of the text must be stored into a one-dimensional array as they are read. Compare E with each element of the array. Each time a match occurs, add one to the count. Print the count in message form.

12. Each record of a set of records contains a person's name, age, and sex—M for male, F for female. There is a header record containing the number of records in the set. Construct a pseudocode program that builds two arrays from the input data—one containing names of males and the other containing names of females. Print the names of males and the names of females with identifying headings. (You will have to count the males as their names are placed into the array; the same is true for the females.)

13. Given two one-dimensional arrays of 20 elements each, containing numbers in the range from −99 to +99, construct a computer program in pseudocode that determines which pairs (if any) add up

to 50. A pair consists of one element from each array. Print headings, the array subscripts, and the element values for each pair whose sum is 50 as follows:

ARRAY 1		ARRAY 2	
SUBSCRIPT	VALUE	SUBSCRIPT	VALUE
12	25	3	25
14	99	5	−49

(Hint: Start with the first element of the first array and pair it with each element of the second array. Then pair the second element of the first array with each element of the second array. Continue in this manner.)

14. Suppose that a line of text is read from a record containing 80 characters. Construct a computer program in pseudocode that counts the number of times each letter of the alphabet occurs in the text, storing the counts in an array. Print the count for each letter with an identifying label. (Hint: Use a second array containing the letters of the alphabet to do the comparisons. Suppose that the first letter of the text is C. It is found in the third position of the array containing the alphabet, so add one to the counter in the third position of the array used for counting.)

15. You are given two one-dimensional arrays of 100 elements each. The first array contains names, and the second contains telephone numbers corresponding to names in the first array. That is, the first name and the first telephone number correspond, and so on. You are also given a set of input records, each containing a name. Construct a computer program in pseudocode that reads each name, finds the position of the name in the array of names, and prints the name and the corresponding phone number. (Assume that each name in the input data is found in the array of names.)

16. Construct a computer program in pseudocode that reverses the order of a one-dimensional array. Do not use a second array; use only one temporary storage location. Remember to account for arrays with an even number of elements and arrays with an odd number of elements and also for arrays of one element.

17. Construct a computer program in pseudocode that sums the elements of a one-dimensional array.

18. Modify exercise 11 so that a text of any length can be read from a set of records, each containing 50 characters. The last character is a dollar sign and will appear in the last position of the last record. Process the text one record at a time, continuing until the last record, indicated by the dollar sign, is encountered.

19. You are given a text of 20 characters. Construct a computer program in pseudocode that places the characters into an array and prints them, and rotates the characters one position to the left and prints them, repeating the process 20 times. By rotation to the left we mean to save the 1st character in a temporary location, move the 2nd character into the 1st position, the 3rd into the 2nd, the 4th into the 3rd, and so on, until all 20 characters have been moved. Then move the character in the temporary location into the 20th position. The printed output will look like the following:

> **THE LORD IS A REFUGE**
> **HE LORD IS A REFUGET**
> **E LORD IS A REFUGETH**
> **LORD IS A REFUGETHE**
>   **and so on**

20. This problem is the same as exercise 19 except that you are to rotate the characters to the right one position at a time. An important difference in the procedure is that you must work from right to left in the array. Move the 20th character into a temporary location, and then move the 19th into the 20th, the 18th into the 19th, and so on. When all 20 characters have been moved, then move the one in the temporary location to the 1st position and print the array. Repeat the procedure 20 times. The following is a sample of the printed output:

> **THE LORD IS A REFUGE**
> **ETHE LORD IS A REFUG**
> **GETHE LORD IS A REFU**
> **UGETHE LORD IS A REF**
>   **and so on**

21. Modify exercise 14 so that the program will read a text of any length from a set of records, if the last character of the last record is a dollar sign. (See also exercise 18.)

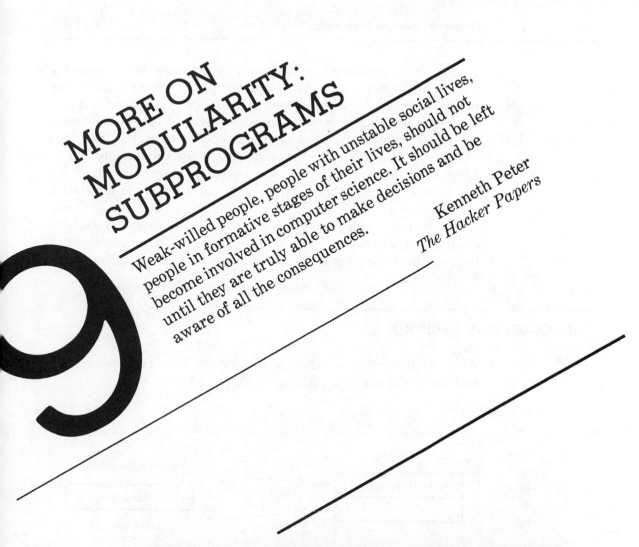

MORE ON MODULARITY: SUBPROGRAMS

Weak-willed people, people with unstable social lives, people in formative stages of their lives, should not become involved in computer science. It should be left until they are truly able to make decisions and be aware of all the consequences.

Kenneth Peter
The Hacker Papers

Modularity in program design was introduced in Chapter 6. A module performs a single subtask. Modules are linked together, or "stacked," so that a module (in general) receives information from the module that precedes it and passes information to the one that follows. In this manner a program is developed to perform a task or some set of tasks.

There are many routine tasks that are common to a variety of problems. For example, integrating a polynomial function is a task that could be encountered in engineering, scientific, mathematical, and business problems. Sorting items of information is another example. Extracting square roots and searching a list for a particular item of information are others.

It seems pointless that when a programmer has designed a module to extract square roots, for example, he or she should have to rewrite that module every time it is needed in a program. It also seems pointless that a second programmer should have to "re-invent the wheel"—that is, design a similar module to extract square roots when he or she needs it. A module that is used repeatedly can be designed so that it can be used when needed simply by "calling" for the module for a program requiring it. Such a module is called a *subprogram*—a program that is subordinate to another program. (It is sometimes called a *procedure*.) Thus, a subprogram is a special kind of module that performs some task or set of tasks and that can be appended to another program as a subtask of that program.

THE CONCEPT OF A SUBPROGRAM

When a subprogram is called from a program, several events must take place. These are summarized in Figure 9-1.

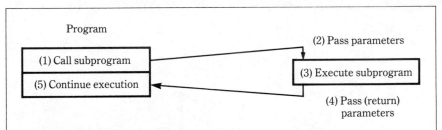

1. A subprogram is *invoked,* or *called,* in the program by its name.

2. The items of information, called *parameters,* necessary for the subprogram to perform its task, are made available, or *passed,* to it.

3. The subprogram performs its task.

4. Results, which are also called *parameters,* are made available, or *passed,* to the program.

5. The program continues execution at the statement that immediately follows the statement that called the subprogram.

Figure 9-1.   The steps in using a subprogram.

THE CALLING PROGRAM

A program that calls or invokes a subprogram is known as a *calling program*. (It is sometimes called a *main program*.)

In pseudocode we use the *call* statement to invoke a subprogram. The general form of the *call* statement is as follows:

> **call** *name* (*list of parameters*)

where *name* is the name of the subprogram and *list of parameters* includes the names or actual values of items of information that must be available to the subprogram. No distinction is made in the parameter list between values sent to and those returned from the subprogram. They are all parameters. The parameter list can be thought of as a bridge between the calling program and the subprogram, making the parameters available to both programs. The subprogram may use the value of any parameter, and it may change or assign the value of any parameter. In other words, a value of a parameter may be used or assigned from either side of the "bridge," and it has that value in both of the programs linked by the "bridge." Figure 9-2 illustrates the "parameter bridge."

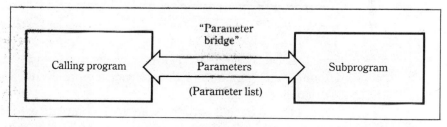

Figure 9-2.   A "parameter bridge" linking a calling program and a subprogram. Values of parameters are available to both programs through the "bridge," which is actually the parameter list.

When a *call* statement is executed, the "parameter bridge" is established, and program control passes to the subprogram so that it can be executed. Program control is returned to the calling program when the subprogram has been completed; execution then resumes at the statement immediately following the *call* statement.

THE SUBPROGRAM

There are two classes of subprograms: internal and external. An *internal subprogram* is contained within and is a part of the calling program. An *external subprogram* is separate from and independent of the calling program. Figure 9-3 illustrates this difference between internal and external subprograms.

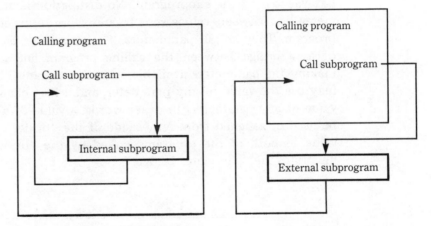

Figure 9-3.   Two classes of subprograms: internal and external.

Because there are fewer complications with regard to the use of names and parameters in external subprograms, we shall focus our discussion on them.

The external subprogram is a complete program independent of the calling program except for its link through the parameter list. When invoked, the subprogram performs the necessary operations, making use of the parameters, and returns control to the calling program when it has completed its processing.

The subprogram is a module that performs one or more subtasks. Like all other modules, the subprogram has one entry (at the top) and one exit (at the bottom).

In pseudocode we introduce a subprogram with a *subprogram* statement. The general form is as follows:

subprogram *name* (*list of parameters*)

where *name* is the name of the subprogram and *list of parameters* includes the names of items of information that must be available to the subprogram. The parameter list in the subprogram must match the parameter list in the *call* statement in (1) number of parameters, (2) order of parameters, and (3) type (array must correspond to array, single value to single value, and so on). This correspondence is illustrated in Figure 9-4.

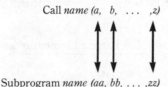

Call *name (a,   b,   . . . ,z)*

Subprogram *name (aa, bb, . . . ,zz)*

Figure 9-4.   Correspondence between the parameter lists of a call *statement and a* subprogram *statement.*

Both lists must have the same number of parameters. The first parameter in the list of the *call* statement in Figure 9-4 corresponds to the first one in the list of the *subprogram* statement, the second to the second, and so on. If *a* is an array, then *aa* must also be an array; if *a* is a single value, then *aa* must be a single value; and so on. These restrictions are reasonable, considering the analogy of the parameter bridge. Values of parameters must be the same from either end of the bridge. The names of the parameters do not have to be the same, however. The first parameter in the calling list (*a*) could be named JACK, for example, and the first parameter in the subprogram list (*aa*) could be JILL. Recall that a calling program and a subprogram are separate, complete programs. Therefore, names used in one have no relationship to those used in the other, apart from their correspondence in parameter lists. (There are exceptions to this statement, as we shall see toward the end of this chapter, when using internal subprograms.)

A *return* or *exit* statement is used at the end of the subprogram. It completes the execution of the subprogram and returns control to the calling program.

THE LARGEST NUMBER PROBLEM

The program in Chapter 8 for finding the largest element in an array is a good program to generalize into a subprogram. The task of finding the largest element in an array is one that we might have occasion to use as a subtask of a number of problems.

In the form of a subprogram, the largest number program can be used with any calling program. IPO Diagram 9-1 shows a subprogram named LARGEST, which finds the largest element in an array.

IPO Diagram 9-1.   Subprogram: The Largest Element in an Array

Input	Process	Output
An array of numbers, N. Number of elements in the array, NUM.	1. Subprogram LARGEST (N, NUM, MAX). 2. Declare N to be an array. 3. Save N(1) in MAX. 4. Loop for J = 2 to NUM. If N(J) > MAX, then save N(J) in MAX. End if. End loop. 5. Return.	Largest element, MAX.

The parameters are listed in the "Input" and "Output" columns. Those that provide information required for performing the subprogram's task are in the "Input" column. Those that are used for the results are in the "Output" column. Thus, in IPO Diagram 9-1 the number of elements in the array (NUM) and the name of the array (N), both of which contain information required by the subprogram in order for it to perform its task, are in the "Input" column. The result, the largest element in the array (MAX), is in the "Output" column.

The parameters are also included in the parameter list in the *subprogram* statement. This further reminds us that they are parameters and specifies their order in the list.

The *return* statement is used at the bottom for returning control to the calling program.

Recall that a subprogram is a complete program, which is separate from the calling program. It is constructed as any program is constructed—except for the *subprogram* statement, which identifies it as a subprogram, and the *return* statement, which appears at the end instead of *stop*. It is necessary, therefore, to declare all arrays that appear in the subprogram, including those in the parameter list.

The subprogram to find the largest element can be used with any program having the required *call* statement. IPO Diagram 9-2 shows such a program. Notice that the name of the array (K) and the number of elements (NUMBER) are not the same as those used in the subprogram (N and NUM, respectively). Recall that the calling program and the subprogram are separate programs and that the names used in one have no relationship to those in the other, except through the parameter list. (We are still discussing external subprograms.) Thus, the array is regarded as N from one end of the parameter bridge and K from the other; both names refer to the same array. Similarly, the number of elements is regarded as NUMBER from one end of the bridge and NUM from the other, both referring to the same value. The largest value happens to be named MAX from both ends of the bridge.

IPO Diagram 9-2.   Calling Program for Subprogram LARGEST

Input	Process	Output
Header record with number of elements in an array of numbers. An array of numbers.	1. Declare K to be an array. 2. Get number of elements NUMBER from header record. 3. Loop for J = 1 to NUMBER. Get K(J). Print 'K(', J, ') = ', K(J). End loop. 4. Call LARGEST (K, NUMBER, MAX). 5. Print 'Largest number is ', MAX. 6. Stop.	Largest number.

Notice the correspondence between the parameter list of the *call* statement and the *subprogram* statement. The two lists agree in number: both have three parameters. The order of the parameters is the same in both lists: array, number of elements, largest element. Finally, the corresponding parameters agree in type: N and K are arrays, NUM and NUMBER are single values, and MAX (calling program) and MAX (subprogram) are single values.

J is used for the value of the counter in the calling program, as well as in the subprogram. Since J is not included in the parameter lists (and LARGEST is an external subprogram), J in the calling program and J in the subprogram have absolutely no relationship.

THE BUBBLE SORT

Sorting is a required subtask of many kinds of problems. Thus, a subprogram to do sorting would be particularly useful. The bubble sort from Chapter 8 can easily be made into a subprogram. (Recall that the bubble sort is inefficient. We would normally choose a more efficient sorting algorithm for a subprogram.) IPO Diagram 9-3 shows a subprogram named BSORT that performs the bubble sort.

IPO Diagram 9-3.   Subprogram: Refined Bubble Sort

Input	Process	Output

An array of numbers, AR.
 	
Number of elements in the array, NUM.
	1. Subprogram BSORT (AR,NUM).
	
	2. Declare AR to be an array.
	
	3. Set LIMIT to $(N-1)$.
	
	4. Set switch to 1.
	
	5. Loop while switch is 1 and LIMIT > 0.
	    Set switch to 0.
	    Loop for J = 1 to LIMIT.
	     If $AR(J) > AR(J+1)$, then interchange $AR(J)$ and $AR(J+1)$.
	
	     Set switch to 1.
	     End if.
	     End loop.
	     Subtract 1 from LIMIT.
	    End loop.
	
	6. Return.
		Array AR arranged in ascending order.

SEARCHING FOR AN ELEMENT IN AN ARRAY

Searching for a particular element of an array is another common subtask that can be made into a subprogram.

Searching an array is a simple concept. We must be given an array, the number of elements in the array, and the item that we want to look for in the array. If we find it, we want to know the location (position, subscript) of that item in the array. If it is not in the array, we want to know that too. (A common example of this kind of search is finding a particular house on a street.)

The process involves comparing each element in the array with the item that we are looking for. If an element *matches*, or is equal to, what we are looking for, we want to stop looking and record the position (subscript) of that element in the array. If the item we are looking for is not found (we have compared it with all elements in the array and found no match), we can record a nonsense value, such as 0 or −1, which cannot possibly be an allowed position number.

IPO Diagram 9-4 shows a subprogram that performs a search on an array.

IPO Diagram 9-4.   Subprogram: Search for Element in Array

Input	Process	Output
An array AR. Number of elements in array, N. Element to be found, FIND.	1. Subprogram SEARCH (AR, N, FIND, LOC). 2. Declare AR to be an array. 3. Set LOC to −1 in case element is not found. 4. Loop for J = 1 to N. If FIND = AR(J), then save position J in LOC. Go to step 5. End if. End loop. 5. Return.	Position of element in array, LOC.

This program contains a new structural concept. Notice that the selection module contains "Go to step 5." The reason for this, of course, is that the search must be terminated when a match is found. Thus, there are two exits from the selection module: one when the item is not found (the normal exit) and one when the item is found (an early exit). This second exit also exits the repetition module, giving it two exits as well. We have maintained in previous chapters that a module has a single exit at the bottom of the module. How can two exits be allowed? The answer is simply that the logic of the process requires this unusual exit, even though it is a departure from established procedure. We can think of this unusual exit as a "sideways" exit, and we will see how to avoid it in a moment.

Figure 9-5 illustrates the structure of the sideways exit in the program in IPO Diagram 9-4.

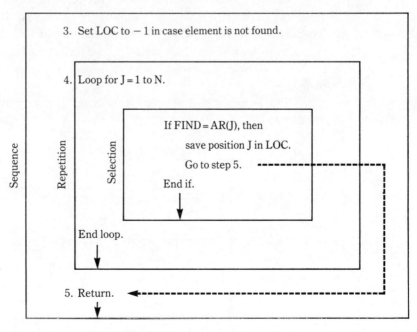

Figure 9-5.   A "sideways" exit from a selection module and a repetition module. This departure from the usual exit at the bottom of a module should be avoided.

A sideways exit is tolerable in exceptional cases when the program logic cannot be expressed as clearly and conveniently with the usual program structures. We should always look for ways to avoid it, however, because it is inconsistent with standard program structure.

Is there an alternate way to construct the loop module for our search algorithm that is equally clear, or perhaps clearer? One possibility appears in IPO Diagram 9-5.

IPO Diagram 9-5. Subprogram: Search for Element in Array Using Proper Constructs

Input	*Process*	*Output*
An array AR. Number of elements in array, N. Element to be found, FIND.	1. Subprogram SEARCH (AR, N, FIND, LOC) 2. Declare AR to be an array. 3. Set J to one. 4. Loop while J ≤ N and FIND ≠ AR(J). 　　Add one to J. End loop. 5. If J > N, then 　　set LOC to −1. [Not found] Else 　　set LOC to J. [Found] End if. 6. Return.	Position of element in array, LOC.

Perform a trace on the program in IPO Diagram 9-5 to verify that it is correct. What happens if N is zero (that is, there are no elements in the array)?

INTERNAL SUBPROGRAMS

The subprograms that have been presented so far in this chapter are of the class referred to as external subprograms. This means that the calling program and the subprogram are separate entities. Neither is a part of or contained in the other. The rules that have been discussed are for external subprograms. Now let us turn our attention to internal subprograms.

Internal subprograms are contained within the calling program and are a part of it. Therefore, names used in an internal subprogram are not necessarily independent of the calling program, and vice versa. A name that is available to both programs is said to be *global*. A name that is available only within one program (the calling program or the internal subprogram) is said to be *local*. A name in a calling program is global to an internal subprogram—unless it is *declared* in the subprogram, which makes it local to the subprogram.

Determining which names are global and local to which programs can be confusing to the beginning programmer. Let us look at an example and identify names that are local and names that are global. We shall also see how parameter lists may be used with internal subprograms.

THE LARGEST NUMBER PROBLEM, USING AN INTERNAL SUBPROGRAM

IPO Diagram 9-2 shows how a calling program for the external subprogram LARGEST from IPO Diagram 9-1 can be used to find the largest number in an array. IPO Diagram 9-6 illustrates how to turn LARGEST into an internal subprogram. We can make several observations regarding the program.

The names K, NUMBER, and MAX in the calling program are global to the subprogram. These names may be used in the subprogram, and they refer to the same values in both programs. MAX is used in the subprogram, but the names K and NUMBER are not. Since MAX is global to both programs, if its value changes in the calling program, it also changes in the subprogram, and vice versa.

The *values* (distinct from the names) of K and NUMBER are used in the subprogram through the parameter list and are renamed N and NUM, respectively, just as they would be in an external subprogram.

Since the names N and NUM are in the subprogram, they are local to it and are not global to the calling program.

J is declared in the subprogram, making it local. Therefore, J in the calling program and J in the subprogram are unrelated. When the value of J changes in the calling program, it does not change in the subprogram, and vice versa.

These observations are summarized in Figure 9-6.

IPO Diagram 9-6.   The Largest Element in an Array, Using an Internal Subprogram.

Input	Process	Output

Header record with number of elements in an array of numbers.
 	
An array of numbers.
	1. Declare K to be an array.
	
	2. Get number of elements NUMBER from header record.
	
	3. Loop for J = 1 to NUMBER.
	    Get K(J).
	    Print 'K(', J, ') = ', K(J).
	End loop.
	
	4. Call LARGEST (K, NUMBER).
	
	5. Print 'Largest number is ', MAX.
	
	6. Stop.
	
	7. Subprogram LARGEST (N, NUM).
	
	8. Declare N to be an array.
	    Declare J.
	
	9. Save N(1) in MAX.
	
	10. Loop for J = 2 to NUM.
	    If N(J) > MAX, then
	      save N(J) in MAX.
	    End if.
	End loop.
	
	11. Return.
		Largest number.

Calling program	Observations	Internal subprogram
K (global)	Linked through parameter list	N (local)
NUMBER (global)	Linked through parameter list	NUM (local)
J (local)	Unrelated	J (local)
MAX (global)	Same	MAX (global)

Figure 9-6.   Relationships between names used in the calling program and names used in the internal subprogram in IPO Diagram 9-6.

Although we have barely touched the subject of internal subprograms, any further discussion is beyond the scope of this book. If you need to know more about them, refer to an appropriate textbook or computer language manual.

FUNCTIONS

There is yet another special class of subprograms called *functions*. (They may be either internal or external.) Most computer languages include certain functions that are commonly used, such as a function to take the square root. Usually provision is also made for the programmer to construct his or her own functions.

Functions are not called explicitly with a *call* statement. They are called implicitly by use of the function name followed by a parameter list as a part of an expression in a statement—for example, an arithmetic expression in an assignment statement.

One value is returned to the calling program from a function, and it is returned as the name of the function. (The parameters in the list may be used just as they are in the general subprogram, however.) A function should be used only in those cases in which the result is a single value. Otherwise, a general subprogram should be used.

A function is introduced in pseudocode by a *function* statement, whose general form is as follows:

function *name* (*list of parameters*)

where *name* is the name of the function and *list of parameters* includes the names of items of information that must be available to the function. A *return* or *exit* statement is placed at the end of the function.

The name of a function must be assigned a value in the function, since the single result is returned to the calling program through the name.

In other respects, the function is like the general subprogram.

The subprogram that finds the largest element in an array (IPO Diagram 9-1) produces a single result—the largest element. Therefore, it can be constructed as a function. IPO Diagram 9-7 shows a function that finds the largest element in an array.

IPO Diagram 9-7.   Function that Finds the Largest Element in an Array

Input	Process	Output
An array of numbers, N. Number of elements in the array, NUM.	1. Function LARGEST (N, NUM). 2. Declare N to be an array. 3. Save N(1) in MAX. 4. Loop for J = 2 to NUM. If N(J) > MAX, then save N(J) in MAX. End if. End loop. 5. Save MAX in LARGEST. 6. Return.	Largest element, MAX.

Notice that the name of the function (LARGEST) is assigned the value of MAX as required, so that the value of MAX can be returned to the calling program (step 5).

IPO Diagram 9-8 shows a calling program for the function.

IPO Diagram 9-8.   Calling Program for Function LARGEST

Input	Process	Output
Header record with number of elements in an array. An array of numbers.	1. Declare K to be an array. 2. Get number of elements NUMBER from header record. 3. Loop for J = 1 to NUMBER. Get K(J). Print 'K(', J, ') = ', K(J). End loop. 4. Set MAX to LARGEST (K, NUMBER). 5. Print 'Largest number is ', MAX. 6. Stop.	Largest number.

EXERCISES

1. Construct a calling program for the bubble sort subprogram (IPO Diagram 9-3). It must input and print the array, call the subprogram, and print the sorted array.

2. Construct a calling program for the search subprogram (IPO Diagram 9-5). It must input and print the array, input and print the item to be found, call the subprogram, and print the position of the item (if found) or a message saying that the item was not found.

3. Repeat exercise 2 using an internal subprogram for the search. Identify local and global names.

4. The subprogram that searches an array for a particular element (IPO Diagram 9-5) returns a single value to the calling program. Construct a function that performs the same task as the subprogram.

5. Construct a calling program for the function in exercise 4.

6. The harmonic mean is defined as follows:

$$H = \frac{n}{\dfrac{1}{x_1} + \dfrac{1}{x_2} + \dfrac{1}{x_3} + \ldots + \dfrac{1}{x_n}} ,$$

where H is the harmonic mean and n is the number of elements in the array x. Construct a function that receives a set of values in the array x and returns the harmonic mean to the calling program. Be sure to place a test in your program so that division by zero will not occur. If an element of the array has a value of zero, set H to zero. (Is zero a nonsense value of H? Can the harmonic mean ever be zero?)

7. Construct a general subprogram to compute the harmonic mean (refer to exercise 6).

8. Construct calling programs for the subprogram in exercise 7 and the function in exercise 6. They must input the array, call the subprogram or function, and print the harmonic mean or a message saying that it is undefined (zero returned from the subprogram or function).

9. Can the bubble sort subprogram (IPO Diagram 9-3) be made into a function? Why?

10. The Fibonacci sequence was described in Chapter 4, exercise 8. Construct a subprogram that receives a number n, generates the first n numbers of the Fibonacci sequence, places them into an array, and returns the array to the calling program.

11. Compare the programs in IPO Diagrams 9-4 and 9-5. Which one do you prefer? Why? Which one is clearer? Why?

12. Modify exercise 11 from Chapter 5 so that a subprogram is used to determine the service charge for each type of checking account. Also, use a subprogram to produce the output.

13. You are given a record containing the number of days a library book is overdue, the name of the person who checked the book out, the name of the book, and the cost to replace the book. Construct a computer program in pseudocode that calculates and prints the fine and prints a "replacement" message if the book is more than 90 days overdue. The fine is equal to five cents per day up to 90 days. Thereafter the fine is the cost to replace the book plus 15% for handling costs. Use one subprogram to calculate the fine, and another to print the appropriate message.

14. Modify exercise 20 from Chapter 5 using a subprogram to calculate the federal income tax. Also use a subprogram to produce the output.

15. Modify exercise 15 from Chapter 8 using one subprogram to search for the matching name, and another to produce the output.

16. Construct a computer program in pseudocode that reads a set of 100 records, each containing a single number, and stores the numbers in an array. Use subprograms to read the stack into the array, search for the second largest number, and print the second largest number.

17. Redo exercise 4 from Chapter 7 using a general subprogram to compute the sum of the first 100 terms of the expression. Also construct a function that performs the same task.

18. Construct a subprogram that finds the first X elements of the Fibonacci sequence (exercise 8 from Chapter 4), where X is some number passed from the calling program.

19. Redo exercise 8 from Chapter 7 using a subprogram that receives the values of m and n from the calling program.

20. Convert exercise 9 from Chapter 7 into a subprogram.

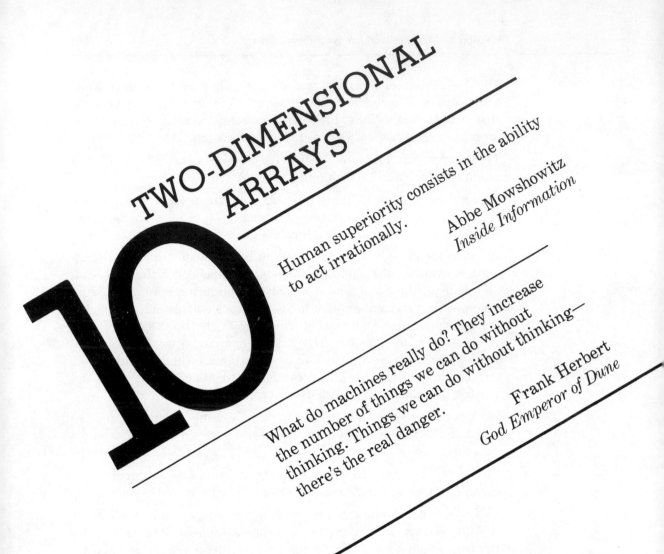

10 TWO-DIMENSIONAL ARRAYS

Human superiority consists in the ability to act irrationally.

Abbe Mowshowitz
Inside Information

What do machines really do? They increase the number of things we can do without thinking. Things we can do without thinking—there's the real danger.

Frank Herbert
God Emperor of Dune

In Chapter 8 we defined an array as any grouping of items that have some similar characteristics or identifying property in common. We identified each element of an array by a positional number called a subscript.

We frequently encounter arrays for which a single positional number is inconvenient. We would much prefer to identify elements by two positional numbers. Let us consider a few examples.

Seats in an auditorium constitute an array. We could simply number them consecutively, as in a one-dimensional array; however, this would make finding a particular seat inconvenient. We much prefer to think of the seats arranged by rows and for each seat to have two positional numbers: a row number and a seat number in that row. A seat might be specified by *row 10 seat 6*, for example.

We could number houses in a city consecutively from some point. However, they are much more easily identified by streets and numbers—two positional designations.

We may even consider people as an array, each element of which has two identifiers: the surname (family name) and the given name. (This analogy quickly breaks down, though, since many people have identical names.)

The calendar is conveniently arranged by months and days, so that we can specify a particular day of a particular month, such as the 6th day of April. (That is the 96th day of a non-leap year, if the year is considered as a one-dimensional array of days.)

We often encounter tables of information. Tables are arranged in rows and columns, making the information easier to read and interpret and particular items in the table easier to find. Each item in the table is uniquely identified by row and column, which are two positional designations.

We shall consider a table of information in detail later in this chapter. First, however, we need to examine arrays with two positional numbers.

TWO-DIMENSIONAL ARRAYS

We used a carton of eggs in Chapter 8 to illustrate the concept of an array. The eggs were assigned positional numbers (subscripts) 1–12. We can also think of the eggs as having two positional numbers: one specifying the row in which an egg is found and the other specifying the column. Figure 10-1 illustrates a two-dimensional array of eggs.

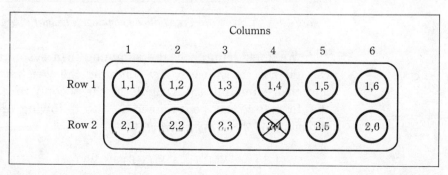

Figure 10-1. Eggs in a carton, viewed as a two-dimensional array. Egg(2,4) is marked with an X.

We can think of each egg in the carton as being in a row and a column of the carton. The egg in row 2, column 4 is marked with an X. The position of each egg is uniquely specified by a row number and a column number. Thus, each position is specified by two positional numbers, or two subscripts; the array is said to be *two dimensional*. (We may think of it as having the dimensions of length and width or height and width.)

Each element in a two-dimensional array must have two subscripts: the row number first, the column number second. (By convention, we always place the row number first.) The egg in row 2, column 4 (Figure 10-1) could then be identified as *egg(2,4)*.

THE AVERAGE WEIGHT OF EGGS IN A CARTON

Figure 10-2 shows the weight of each egg in a carton. Let us find the average weight of the eggs. (Weights are in grams.)

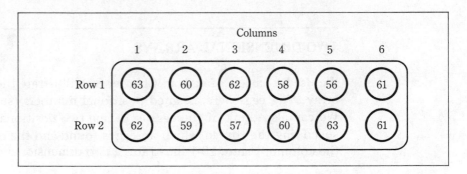

Figure 10-2.   Carton of eggs, showing each egg's weight in grams.

We must approach the summing in a systematic manner. We can do this most easily by summing the weights in the first row and then summing the weights in the second row. The weights in the first row can be summed in the following order, where W is the name of the array of weights:

$$W(1,1) \quad W(1,2) \quad W(1,3) \quad W(1,4) \quad W(1,5) \quad W(1,6).$$

Notice that the first subscript, the row number, is set to 1 and remains constant. The second subscript, the column number, starts with 1 and ends with 6.

The weights in the second row can be summed in the following order:

$$W(2,1) \quad W(2,2) \quad W(2,3) \quad W(2,4) \quad W(2,5) \quad W(2,6).$$

Again, the row number remains constant at 2, while the column number takes on values 1-6.

It should be clear that we need two counters for summing the elements of W: a counter for the row number, which takes on the values 1 and 2, and a counter for the column number, which takes the values 1-6. The row counter counts once for every six counts of the column counter. Figure 10-3 illustrates this.

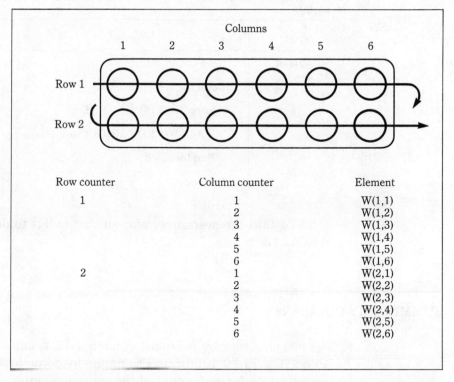

Figure 10-3. The weights of the eggs are summed by rows—the first row, followed by the second row. The column counter takes on values 1-6 for each row.

IPO Diagram 10-1 shows a module for summing the weights. The name of the row counter is KROW, while the name of the column counter is KCOL. We have *nested* loops, each of which is a *loop with counter*. KROW of the outer loop is set to 1, and the body of the loop is executed. But the body is another *loop with counter* module. Therefore, KCOL of the inner loop is set to 1, and the body of the inner loop is executed: W(1,1) is added to the sum. Then KCOL is set to 2, and W(1,2) is added. This continues until W(1,6) has been added. A normal exit is taken from the inner loop, causing KROW of the outer loop to be set to 2. The body of the outer loop, which is the inner loop, is executed again. KCOL is set to 1, and W(2,1) is added. This continues until W(2,6) has been added. A normal exit occurs from the inner loop, followed by a normal exit from the outer loop. The summing is completed.

IPO Diagram 10-1. Summing the Elements of a Two-Dimensional Array by Rows

Input	Process	Output

Weights of 12 eggs in an array W.	Set SUM to 0.
	
	 Loop for KROW = 1 to 2.
	
	   Loop for KCOL = 1 to 6.
	
	     Add W(KROW,KCOL) to SUM.
	
	   End loop.
	
	 End loop.
		Sum of elements in array W.

To find the average weight, all that is left to do is to divide the sum by 12.

SUMMING BY COLUMNS

We can also sum by columns: column 1 first, column 2 second, and so on. Figure 10-4 illustrates summing by columns. The row counter counts twice for each count of the column counter.

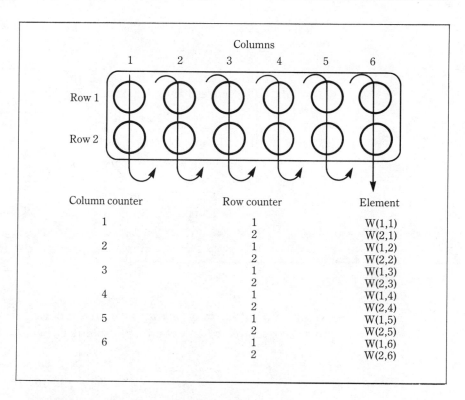

Figure 10-4.   The weights of the eggs are summed by columns. The row counter takes on values 1–2 for each column.

IPO Diagram 10-2 shows a module for summing the weights by columns. KCOL of the outer loop is set to 1, and the body of the loop is executed. KROW of the inner loop is set to 1, and the body of the inner loop is executed. W(1,1) is added. Then KROW is set to 2, and W(2,1) is added. A normal exit is taken from the inner loop, causing KCOL of the outer loop to be set to 2. The body of the outer loop, which is the inner loop, is executed again, adding W(1,2) and W(2,2). A normal exit from the inner loop causes KCOL of the outer loop to be set to 3, and the process continues until W(2,6), the last element, has been added. A normal exit is taken from the inner loop, followed by a normal exit from the outer loop, and the summing is completed.

IPO Diagram 10-2. Summing the Elements of a Two-Dimensional Array by Columns

Input	Process	Output
Weights of 12 eggs in an array W.	Set SUM to 0. Loop for KCOL = 1 to 6. Loop for KROW = 1 to 2. Add W(KROW,KCOL) to SUM. End loop. End loop.	Sum of elements in array W.

A TABLE OF INFORMATION

A simple inventory may be displayed in a tabular format. Figure 10-5 shows an example of an inventory of pants by waist size.

	28	30	32	34	36	38	40
Jeans	3	5	8	10	9	12	7
Slacks	0	16	20	35	10	13	21
Shorts	1	4	9	16	8	10	4

Figure 10-5.   A simple inventory. The table shows the number of each type of pants by waist size.

Suppose that we want to use a computer program to find the total number of each type of pants and also the total number of items of each waist size. To find the total number of jeans, for example, we must add the numbers in the "Jeans" row. But to find the total number of items of waist size 32, we must add all numbers in the column headed "32." In other words, we solve the problem by processing it as a two-dimensional array—by adding the numbers by rows (that is, a row at a time) to find the totals by type of pants, and by columns (that is, a column at a time) to find the totals by waist size. Furthermore, we can conveniently place the totals of the rows in an additional column to the right of the table and place the totals by waist size in an additional row at the bottom of the table. Figure 10-6 shows the table with the row and column numbered and the types and waist sizes removed.

Columns

	1	*2*	*3*	*4*	*5*	*6*	*7*	*8*
1	3	5	8	10	9	12	7	
2	0	16	20	35	10	13	21	
3	1	4	9	16	8	10	4	
4								

Rows (label to the left of rows 2–3)

Figure 10-6. The inventory of pants in the format of a two-dimensional array. Row totals will be placed in column 8, and column totals will be placed in row 4.

The problem, then, is to fill in the blank areas of the table by summing down the columns and across the rows. (The bottom-right position, row 4 and column 8, will contain a grand total of all items.)

IPO Diagram 10-3 shows a module for finding the sums of the rows and placing them in their respective positions in column 8.

IPO Diagram 10-3. Summing the Rows of the Inventory Array

Input	*Process*	*Output*
Two-dimensional array containing three rows and seven columns of numbers.	(Declare INVENTORY to be an array with four rows and eight columns.) Loop for KROW = 1 to 3. Set SUM to 0. Loop for KCOL = 1 to 7. Add INVENTORY(KROW,KCOL) to SUM. End loop. Save SUM in INVENTORY(KROW,8). End loop.	Sums of rows in column 8.

Figure 10-7 illustrates the summing process. The sum of the first row is placed in position (1,8), the sum of the second row in position (2,8), and the sum of the third in position (3,8).

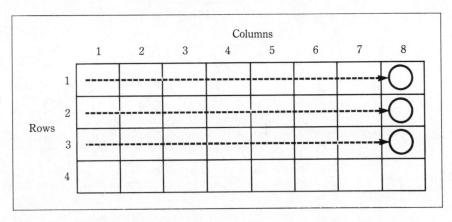

Figure 10-7. Summing across the rows. The circles in column 8 represent the sums of the rows.

IPO Diagram 10-4 shows a module for finding the sums of the columns and placing them in row 4. There are now eight columns to be summed, since we want to find the grand total of all items and place it in position (4,8). Figure 10-8 illustrates the process of summing by columns.

IPO Diagram 10-4.   Summing the Columns of the Inventory Array

Input	Process	Output
Two-dimensional array containing three rows and eight columns of numbers.	(Declare INVENTORY to be an array with four rows and eight columns.) Loop for KCOL = 1 to 8. 　Set SUM to 0. 　Loop for KROW = 1 to 3. 　　Add INVENTORY(KROW,KCOL) to SUM. 　End loop. 　Save SUM in INVENTORY(4,KCOL). End loop.	Sums of rows in column 8.

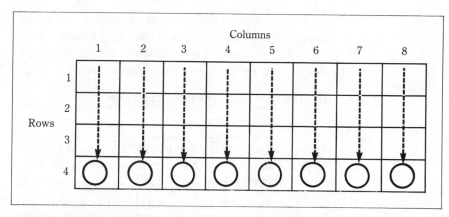

Figure 10-8. Summing down the columns. The circles in row 4 represent the sums of the columns.

The two modules that find the required sums produce a two-dimensional array with the correct information in it. However, in order for a table to be printed in a neat, readable, and easily understood format, we must make some provision for the column headings and the row labels.

The column headings are no problem at all. They can be printed just as we have been printing them all along. But the row labels pose a new problem. We can probably handle them most easily by actually placing them into the array along with the numbers. This is not at all difficult to do, but it does increase our "housekeeping" problems.

Let us define a new array consisting of nine columns, the first of which will contain the row labels. (In some computer programming languages, this column may have to be divided into several columns. For simplicity we will assume that each row label can be contained in a single column.) Figure 10-9 shows this new array.

Columns

	1	2	3	4	5	6	7	8	9
1	JEANS	3	5	8	10	9	12	7	
2	SLACKS	0	16	20	35	10	13	21	
3	SHORTS	1	4	9	16	8	10	4	
4									

Rows

Figure 10-9. The inventory table in the format of a two-dimensional array that includes row labels.

With the array structured in this new fashion, we must sum using only columns 2–9 and omitting column 1.

IPO Diagram 10-5 shows a program for producing a table for the inventory problem that looks like the one in Figure 10-10. We

IPO Diagram 10-5.   The Inventory Table

Input	Process	Output

Three inventory records with one row of table per record.	Declare INVENTORY to be an array with four rows and nine columns.
	
	(Input table.)
	
	Loop for KROW = 1 to 3.
	  Get INVENTORY(KROW, columns 1–8).
	
	End loop.
	
	(Sum by rows; place sums in column 9.)
	
	Loop for KROW = 1 to 3.
	  Set SUM to 0.
	  Loop for KCOL = 2 to 8.
	    Add INVENTORY(KROW,KCOL) to SUM.
	  End loop.
	  Save SUM in INVENTORY(KROW,9).
	
	End loop.
	
	(Sum by columns; place sums in row 4.)
	
	Loop for KCOL = 2 to 9.
	  Set SUM to 0.
	  Loop for KROW = 1 to 3.
	    Add INVENTORY(KROW,KCOL) to SUM.
	  End loop.
	  Save SUM in INVENTORY(4,KCOL).
	
	End loop.
	
	(Output table.)
	
	Save 'TOTAL' in INVENTORY(4,1).
	
	Print table headings.
	
	Loop for KROW = 1 to 4.
	  Print INVENTORY(KROW, columns 1–9).
	
	End loop.
	
	Stop.
		Inventory table in Figure 10-10.

will assume that the table can be read for input so that one input record contains one line of the table. Columns 1–8 and rows 1–3 will be filled on input. Row 4 and column 9 must be filled by the program. The output will consist of the table in Figure 10-10.

	WAIST SIZE							
ITEM	*28*	*30*	*32*	*34*	*36*	*38*	*40*	*TOTAL*
JEANS	3	5	8	10	9	12	7	54
SLACKS	0	16	20	35	10	13	21	115
SHORTS	1	4	9	16	8	10	4	52
TOTAL	4	25	37	61	27	35	32	221

Figure 10-10. Output table for the inventory problem.

USE OF TWO-DIMENSIONAL ARRAYS IN PROGRAMMING LANGUAGES

Programming languages usually include some provision for convenient I/O of two-dimensional arrays. *Indexed I/O lists* is a term sometimes used for this.

Storage of character information in an array with numeric information, as shown in Figure 10-9, can be done in some languages but not in others. A separate one-dimensional array for the labels may be required.

There is a limit to the number of characters that can be stored in an array position in some languages. If the maximum number of characters is four, for example, the array in Figure 10-9 would have to be organized as shown in Figure 10-11.

		Columns									
		1	2	3	4	5	6	7	8	9	10
	1	JEAN	S	3	5	8	10	9	12	7	54
Rows	2	SLAC	KS	0	16	20	35	10	13	21	115
	3	SHOR	TS	1	4	9	16	8	10	4	52
	4	TOTA	L	4	25	37	61	27	35	32	221

Figure 10-11. *Restructuring of the inventory table to accommodate a language that allows a maximum of four characters per array position.*

EXERCISES

1. Modify the program in IPO Diagram 10-5 so that it can process the array shown in Figure 10-11.

2. The sum of two two-dimensional arrays, both with n rows and m columns, is defined to be a two-dimensional array with n rows and m columns, each element of which is the sum of the two elements in the same relative positions of the original arrays. For example, if we want the sum C of arrays A and B, then C (1,1) is A(1,1) + B(1,1); C(1,2) is A(1,2) + B(1,2); and so on. Construct a pseudocode program that will compute the sum of two 5-by-10 arrays (5 rows by 10 columns).

3. In order to produce the table in Figure 10-10, is it necessary to sum the rows before the columns? Construct a pseudocode program that sums the columns first and then the rows. (How will you get the sum into position (4,9)?)

4. The following table shows four models of automobiles, followed by their respective mileage figures for city and highway driving.

Model	City	Highway
Z-34	26.3	41.8
A-46	21.2	35.3
X-11	25.1	38.2
C-20	27.3	37.7

Construct a pseudocode program that computes the average city mileage and the average highway mileage for all four cars. Print a new table that looks like the following table.

Model	City	Highway
Z-34	26.3	41.8
A-46	21.2	35.3
X-11	25.1	38.2
C-20	27.3	37.7
Average	25.0	38.5

5. Using the first table from exercise 4 as input, construct a pseudocode program that computes the unweighted average of city and highway mileage for each model. Print a new table that looks like the following table.

Model	City	Highway	Average
Z-34	26.3	41.8	34.1
A-46	21.2	35.3	28.3
X-11	25.1	38.2	31.7
C-20	27.3	37.7	32.5

6. Construct a subprogram to find the largest element in an m by n array.

7. Construct a computer program in pseudocode to find the second largest element in an m by n array. (One way would be to find the largest element first and eliminate it; then find the largest element of the remaining elements.)

8. Construct a subprogram that sums the contents of an m by n array.

9. Construct a subprogram that prints an m by n array in reverse row-order. That is, row m is printed first, row $m-1$ is printed second, and so on, until row 1 is printed. Be certain that the subprogram works for m and n equal to one.

10. Construct a computer program in pseudocode that "zeroes out" an m by n array. To zero out the array, subtract each element from itself.

11. Construct a subprogram that interchanges the rows and columns of an m by n array. That is, row 1 becomes column 1, row 2 becomes column 2, and so on. (The resulting array is an n by m array.)

12. Redo exercise 15 in Chapter 8 using a 100 by 2 array for the "phone book."

13. A tax table consists of n categories of taxpayers (columns) and m categories of taxable incomes (rows). Construct a subprogram in pseudocode to read the tax table into an m by n array.

14. Construct a computer program in pseudocode that produces a sales report for a six-month period for Fred's Auto Sales, Inc. Use an m by 10 array for storing the data, where m is the number of sales personnel to be represented in the report. Use the first two columns for the name of each salesman, columns 3–8 for the total sales for each month, column 9 for the total sales, and column 10 for the commission. The commission is 5% for all sales below $10,000, 10% for sales from $10,000 to $25,000, and 25% for any sales totaling more than $25,000. Print a report with headings from the array. For three sales personnel the array might appear like the following.

JOHN	SON	1000	2300	5500	7555	9000	1005	26360	6590
MAX		100	105	9000	125	435	465	10230	1023
FRED		9000	9000	9000	9000	9000	9999	54999	13750

The input data are supplied on a set of records, one for each salesman. The header record contains the number of sales personnel. Each sales record contains a name and total sales for each of six months.

15. Construct a computer program in pseudocode that computes a table of squares and square roots. Create the table in an m by 3 array, where m is the number of items to be squared. Read m and all items to be squared and whose square roots are to be found from input records. After m is read, you will be able to use a *loop with counter* to read and process the data. The table should appear as follows for 16, 25, and 64.

16	4	256
25	5	625
64	8	4096

Print the table with appropriate headings.

16. Construct a computer program in pseudocode that creates a simple bar graph for a single salesman from Fred's Auto Sales, Inc. (See exercise 14.) Use a two-dimensional array and let each row represent $1000 in sales. Fill each bar with X's. Print the array with headings. A sample graph for Mr. Johnson follows.

A GRAPH OF SALES FOR JOHNSON

SALES						
10000						
9000					X	
8000					X	
7000				X	X	
6000				X	X	
5000			X	X	X	
4000			X	X	X	
3000			X	X	X	
2000		X	X	X	X	
1000	X	X	X	X	X	X
0	X	X	X	X	X	X
MONTH	1	2	3	4	5	6

17. Modify exercise 16 so that the rows can represent any amount (100s, 1000s, 10s, and so on). Make the graph work for a 12-month period and list the months (use three-letter abbreviations) below the appropriate columns.

18. Modify exercise 15 so that each datum will be raised to the nth power and the nth root extracted. (The nth root is found by raising the datum to the $1/n$th power). Read n, m, and the data from records.

19. Modify exercise 12 from chapter 5, adding to each record a code to indicate the person's age group:

1	less than 20
2	21 through 30
3	31 through 40
4	41 through 65
5	over 65

Use a 5 by 5 array for counting. Print the results in the following form:

AGE	NETWORK
UNDER 20	ZNN
21 – 30	ZBS
31 – 40	YNN
41 – 65	NBZ
OVER 65	ABZ

20. Modify exercise 19 so that the results are presented as percentages of viewers from each age group that watch each network. A sample output with hypothetical results follows:

PERCENTAGE OF VIEWERS BY AGE

AGE	ABZ	NBZ	YNN	ZBS	ZNN
UNDER 20	30	25	2	31	12
21 – 30	20	16	16	18	30
31 – 40	38	18	20	20	4
41 – 65	20	17	3	40	20
OVER 65	10	10	10	50	20

APPENDIX I
ANSI FORTRAN:
1966 AND 1977 STANDARDS

SELECTION WITH THE 1966 STANDARD

The 1966 Standard Fortran does not include an *if-then-else* construct. Selection must therefore be improvised using available statements. The word *Fortran* as used in the following discussion refers to 1966 Standard Fortran.

In Fortran there are three types of selection: logical IF (two-way selection), arithmetic IF (three-way selection), and computed and assigned GO TOs (*n*-way selection).

The conventional construct for two-way selection is the *if-then-else* construct; however, Fortran's two-way selection statement, the logical IF, does not match the general case of the *if-then-else*. Therefore, the *test-false-true* has been devised to overcome this problem. Although it departs somewhat from the *if-then-else* construct, it preserves the sense of two-way selection and at the same time matches the structure of the logical IF.

The general form of the *test* construct for two-way selection is shown in Figure I-1 with its corresponding Fortran code. A CONTINUE statement is used as the exit from the construct. If the selection has a null alternative (one containing no statements), the test must be constructed so that the *true* case is the null one, as shown in Figure I-2. Finally, if there is a null case and the other case consists of a single statement, the logical IF may be used in the usual manner. A simple conditional counter is an example of this.

Pseudocode: If ID is 2, then count.

Fortran: IF (ID .EQ. 2) KOUNT = KOUNT + 1

Test condition.

False. | Sequence for false case |

True. | Sequence for true case |

End test.

```
C --- TEST condition.
      IF (condition) GO TO s
C ---      FALSE. Description of action.
```

| Sequence for false case |

```
                  GO TO t
C ---      TRUE. Description of action.
```

| Sequence for true case |

```
      s     | Sequence for true case |
      t   CONTINUE
C --- END TEST
```

Figure I-1. General two-way selection: pseudocode and Fortran code, where s *and* t *are statement numbers.*

Test condition.

False. | Sequence for false case |

End test.

```
C --- TEST condition.
      IF (condition) GO TO s
C ---     FALSE. Description of action.
```

| Sequence for false case |

```
    s CONTINUE
C --- END TEST
```

Figure I-2. Two-way selection with a null case: pseudocode and Fortran code, where s is a statement number.

The *test* construct can be generalized for three-way selection—the arithmetic IF in Fortran. This is shown in Figure I-3. Any null case is simply omitted.

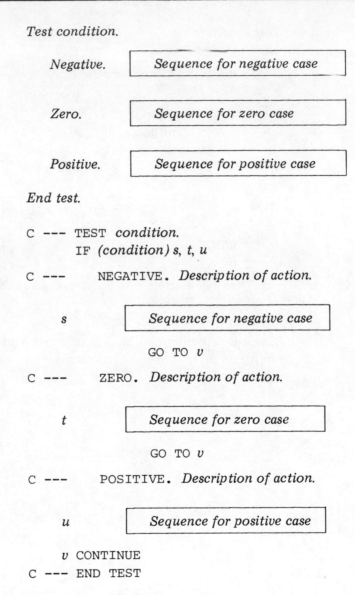

Test condition.

Negative. | Sequence for negative case |

Zero. | Sequence for zero case |

Positive. | Sequence for positive case |

End test.

```
C --- TEST condition.
      IF (condition) s, t, u
C ---      NEGATIVE. Description of action.

    s       | Sequence for negative case |

            GO TO v
C ---      ZERO. Description of action.

    t       | Sequence for zero case |

            GO TO v
C ---      POSITIVE. Description of action.

    u       | Sequence for positive case |

    v  CONTINUE
C --- END TEST
```

Figure I-3. Three-way selection: pseudocode and Fortran code, where s, t, u, *and* v *are statement numbers.*

The *test* construct can be further generalized for *n*-way selection, using the computed GO TO or the assigned GO TO. (The assigned GO TO, whose pseudocode is essentially the same as that for the computed GO TO, will not be discussed here.) Figure I-4 shows the *n*-way selection construct.

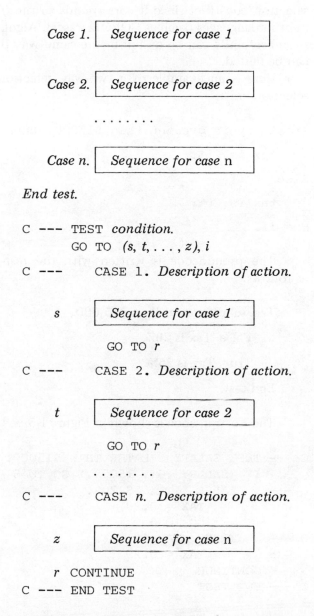

Figure I-4. N way selection: pseudocode and Fortran code, where r, s, t, ..., and z are statement numbers and i is the index. (The assigned GO TO may also be used in the Fortran code.)

Students should generally be encouraged to use the two-way selection construct since it corresponds to the *if-then-else* construct in other languages (such as COBOL, Pascal, Algol, and PL/1).

Test units can be nested in the same way that *if-then-else* units can be nested.

Here is an example of a two-way selection in Fortran for the selection unit:

```
If salary is greater than $15000, then

    tax is 25%.

Else

    tax is 20%.

End if.
```

The pseudocode is written with the *test-false-true* construct as follows:

Test salary greater than $15,000.

> **False. Tax is 20%.**

> **True. Tax is 25%.**

End test.

The Fortran code is shown in Figure I-5.

```
C --- TEST SALARY GREATER THAN $15000.
      IF (SALARY .GT. 15000.) GO TO 5
C ---     FALSE.  TAX IS 20%.
              TAX = 0.20
              GO TO 6
C ---     TRUE.  TAX IS 25%.
      5       TAX = 0.25
      6 CONTINUE
C --- END TEST
```

Figure I-5. Example of a selection unit implemented with the logical IF.

SELECTION WITH THE 1977 STANDARD

Implementation of the *if-then-else* construct in Fortran 77 is straight-forward since Fortran 77 provides an IF-THEN-ELSE statement. The pseudocode is as follows:

If salary is greater than $15,000, then

   tax is 25%.

Else

   tax is 20%.

End if.

This is written in Fortran 77 as follows:

```
IF (SALARY .GT. 15000.) THEN
    TAX = 0.25
ELSE
    TAX = 0.20
END IF
```

REPETITION WITH FORTRAN: BOTH STANDARDS

Neither Fortran 66 nor Fortran 77 provides a *loop while* construct or a *loop until* construct. Therefore, the general loop must be used to simulate these constructs.

The general form of the *loop while* in Fortran is shown in Figure I-6, and the general form of the *loop until* is in Figure I-7.

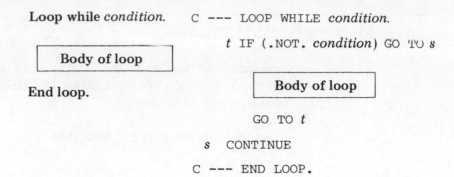

Figure I-6. General form of the loop while *construct in pseudocode and Fortran, where* s *and* t *are statement numbers.*

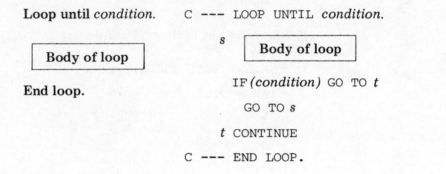

Figure I-7. General form of the loop until *construct in pseudocode and Fortran, where* s *and* t *are statement numbers.*

The general loop is easily implemented in Fortran, as shown in Figure I-8.

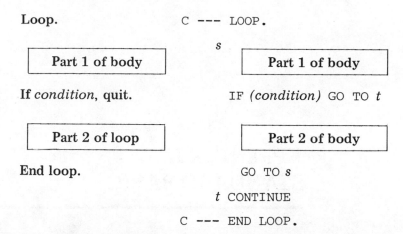

Figure I-8. *The general loop construct in pseudocode and Fortran, where* s *and* t *are statement numbers. Either part 1 or part 2 of the body of the loop may be null.*

Fortran provides the DO loop for the *loop with counter* construct. In many versions of Fortran 66, the loop test is at the bottom; in others it is at the top. In Fortran 77, however, the loop test is at the top. Figure I-9 shows the general form of the *loop with counter*.

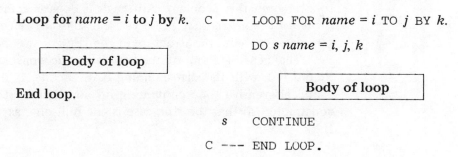

Figure I-9. *General form of* loop with counter *in pseudocode and Fortran, where* s *is a statement number;* name *is the index or counter; and* i, j, *and* k *are the initial, test, and increment values, respectively.*

APPENDIX II
STANDARD BASIC

SELECTION WITH STANDARD BASIC

Some versions of BASIC do not include an *if-then-else* construct. Selection must therefore be improvised using the IF statement.

The conventional construct for selection is the *if-then-else* construct; however, BASIC's IF does not match the general case of the *if-then-else*. Therefore, the *test-false-true* has been devised to overcome this problem. Although it departs somewhat from the *if-then-else* construct, it preserves the sense of selection and at the same time matches the structure of the IF.

The general form of the *test-false-true* construct is shown in Figure II-1 with its corresponding BASIC code. If the selection has a null alternative (one containing no statements), the test must be constructed so that the *true* case is the null one, as shown in Figure II-2.

Test *condition.*

False. | Sequence for false case |

True. | Sequence for true case |

End test.

```
100    REM--TEST condition.
110        IF condition THEN 220
120    REM--    FALSE. Description of action.

130        | Sequence for false case |

200        GO TO 310
210    REM--    TRUE. Description of action.

220        | Sequence for true case |

300    REM--END TEST
310        . . .
```

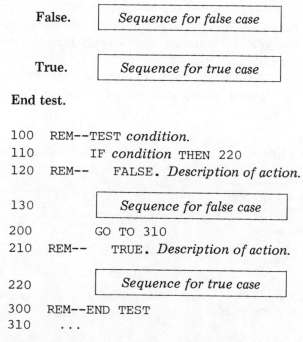

Figure II-1. Selection unit: pseudocode and BASIC code.

Test *condition.*

False. | Sequence for false case |

End test.

```
100    REM--TEST condition.
110        IF condition THEN 210
120    REM--    FALSE. Description of action.

130        | Sequence for false case |

200    REM--END TEST
210        . . .
```

Figure II-2. Selection unit with null true *case: pseudocode and BASIC code.*

Test-false-true units can be nested in the same way that *if-then-else* units can be nested.

REPETITION WITH STANDARD BASIC

Standard BASIC does not provide a *loop while* or a *loop until* construct. Therefore, the general loop must be used to simulate these constructs.

The general form of the *loop while* in standard BASIC is shown in Figure II-3, and the general form of the *loop until* is in Figure II-4.

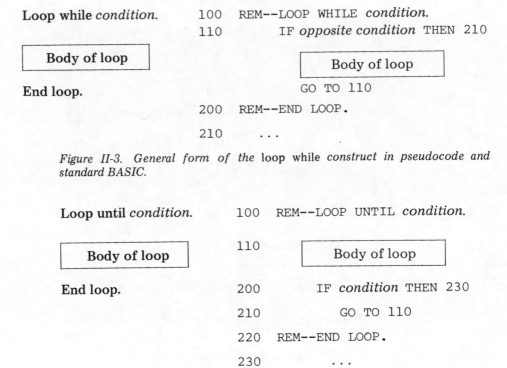

Figure II-3. General form of the loop while *construct in pseudocode and standard BASIC.*

Loop until *condition.*   100   REM--LOOP UNTIL *condition.*

Body of loop	110

End loop.   200   IF *condition* THEN 230

210   GO TO 110

220   REM--END LOOP.

230   . . .

Figure II-4. General form of the loop until *construct in pseudocode and standard BASIC.*

The general loop is easily implemented in standard BASIC, as shown in Figure II-5.

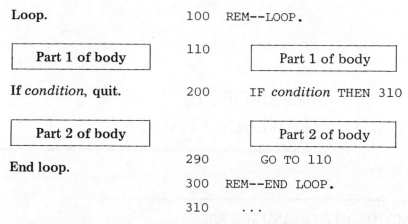

Loop.   100   REM--LOOP.

| **Part 1 of body** | 110 | Part 1 of body |

If *condition*, **quit.**   200   IF *condition* THEN 310

| **Part 2 of body** | | Part 2 of body |

End loop.   290   GO TO 110

                                    300   REM--END LOOP.

                                    310   . . .

Figure II-5. The general loop construct in pseudocode and standard BASIC. Either part 1 or part 2 of the body of the loop may be null.

Standard BASIC provides the FOR/NEXT loop for the *loop with counter* construct. Figure II-6 shows the general form of this construct.

Loop for *name*   100   REM--LOOP FOR *name* = *i* TO *j* BY *k*
  = *i* **to** *j* **by** *k*.
                                    110   FOR *name* = *i* TO *j* STEP *k*

| **Body of loop** | | Body of loop |

End loop.   200   NEXT *name*

                                    210   REM--END LOOP.

                                    220   . . .

Figure II-6. General form of loop with counter *in pseudocode and standard BASIC, where* name *is the index or counter, and* i, j, *and* k *are the initial, test, and increment values, respectively.*

APPENDIX III
STANDARD PASCAL

SELECTION WITH STANDARD PASCAL

The *if-then-else* construct is implemented in Pascal with the IF statement, whose operation corresponds exactly to the *if-then-else* in pseudocode. The general form of the IF statement appears in Figure III-1. Either statement may be a compound statement bracketed by BEGIN and END, as shown in Figure III-2. In the case of a null ELSE (that is, the ELSE case contains no statements), the ELSE portion of the IF is omitted, as in Figure III-3.

```
IF condition THEN
     statement
ELSE
     statement
```

Figure III-1.   The general form of the Pascal IF statement.

```
IF condition THEN
      BEGIN
         statement;
         statement;
            . . .
         statement
      END
ELSE
      BEGIN
         statement;
         statement;
            . . .
         statement
      END
```

Figure III-2.   The general form of the Pascal IF with compound statements.

```
IF condition THEN                    IF condition THEN
      statement                            BEGIN
                                              statement;
                                              statement;
                                                 . . .
                                              statement
                                           END
```

Figure III-3.   The general form of the Pascal IF with a null ELSE, with a single statement and a compound statement.

IF statements may be nested in Pascal.

REPETITION WITH STANDARD PASCAL

Pascal provides a great deal of flexibility in constructing loops, implementing the *loop while*, the *loop until*, and the *loop with counter* constructs.

The *loop while* is implemented with the WHILE DO statement. The general form of the WHILE DO appears in Figure III-4. The body of the loop may be a single statement or a compound statement. The loop test is at the top in the WHILE DO.

```
WHILE condition DO                WHILE condition DO
        statement                         BEGIN
                                              statement;
                                              statement;
                                                  . . .
                                              statement
                                          END
```

Figure III-4. The general form of the WHILE DO with a single statement and a compound statement in the body of the loop.

The *loop until* is implemented with the REPEAT UNTIL statement whose general form appears in Figure III-5. The loop test is at the bottom. This is emphasized in Pascal by the placement of the UNTIL *condition* after the body of the loop.

```
REPEAT                            REPEAT
        statement                         BEGIN
UNTIL condition                               statement;
                                              statement;
                                                  . . .
                                              statement
                                          END
                                  UNTIL condition
```

Figure III-5. The general form of the REPEAT UNTIL with a single statement and a compound statement in the body of the loop.

The *loop with counter* is implemented with the FOR DO statement whose general form appears in Figure III-6. The loop test is at the top. If the TO option is used, the value of the index is incremented (increased) by one after each pass. Looping continues until the value of the index exceeds the test value.

If the DOWNTO option is used, the value of the index is decremented (decreased) by one after each pass. Looping continues until the value of the index is less than the test value. Pascal permits only increments of +1 and −1 in the FOR DO loop.

$$\text{FOR } j := n \left\{ \begin{array}{l} \text{TO} \\ \text{DOWNTO} \end{array} \right\} m \text{ DO} \qquad \text{FOR } j := n \left\{ \begin{array}{l} \text{TO} \\ \text{DOWNTO} \end{array} \right\} m \text{ DO}$$

statement

BEGIN
statement;
statement;
. . .
statement
END

Figure III-6. The general form of the FOR DO loop, where j *is the index or counter,* n *is the initial value, and* m *is the test value. The body of the loop may contain a single statement or a compound statement.*

Index